The Book of the Passion

The Book of the Passion

JOSÉ MIGUEL IBÁÑEZ LANGLOIS

*Translated by David M. Billikopf
and Karin Jürgensen E.*

RESOURCE *Publications* · Eugene, Oregon

THE BOOK OF THE PASSION

Resource Publications
An Imprint of Wipf and Stock Publishers
199 W. 8th Ave., Suite 3
Eugene, OR 97401

www.wipfandstock.com

PAPERBACK ISBN: 978-1-7252-9820-0
HARDCOVER ISBN: 978-1-7252-9819-4
EBOOK ISBN: 978-1-7252-9821-7

07/01/21

Contents

i   1

ii   4

I.   The Final Days   7

II.   The Last Supper   22

III.   The Agony in the Garden   36

IV.   The Jewish Trial   50

V.   The Roman Trial   61

VI.   The Via Crucis   73

VII.   The Seven Words   86

VIII.   Death   99

IX.   The Resurrection   109

*The Word became flesh and
made his dwelling among us.*

JOHN 1:14

*God made him who had no sin to be sin
for us, so that in him we might become
the righteousness of God.*

2 CORINTHIANS 5:21

i

Jesus of Nazareth what a poor fellow
what a total failure
his only disciples some local fishermen
as was to be expected from such simpletons
there was no way to make them understand his purpose
nonetheless with them he journeyed throughout Judea
arousing in the masses a shallow and sporadic exaltation
a tenuous fluttering in the dust of lonely hamlets
as very often happens with migratory preachers
his kith and kin did not believe in him
they thought him mad and so did all the others
defeated by a caste of politicians and divines of his own people
his disciples then abandoned him at midnight
while all the roosters of Jerusalem with neither rhyme nor reason
crowed in unison
sold for 30 dollars cash and not one shekel more
he was condemned as blasphemer impostor revolutionary
by the clamor of that mob supposed to be his brethren
in the shadow of the cross almost no one of his own
just his mother and some youthful followers
those who never fail to hang around the most illuminated dreamers
just some youngsters to scare away the dogs who came to lap his
blood
even his tattered rags were drawn by lot among the soldiers
he passed through this world as though nobody had passed
hours after his death everything in the universe remained the same

only the INRI flickered like a sign upon his blood
a harsh warning to all madmen who pretend to be kings
never was there a man so dead as this man dead upon the cross
his death was as deep as an infinite
Jesus what man so dead

                     so supernatural
souls surrendered to him after his death
the gallows cross was turned into his triumph
the dead leaped forth to love him and adore him
sitting on the sermon of the mount
in a flash his gaze transformed the course of history
leading it along the edge of the most incredible precipices
the so-called course of human history
does nothing but revolve about his person world without end
does nothing else than plunge into the chasm of his heart
his secret voice of archaic Galilean accent
reverberated like a thunderclap dimming the sound of all the
                                                    Caesars
the wisemen and philosophers
his word enlightened everything from inside out
shook human thought with splendors of an unknown light
which the passage of the centuries has not deciphered yet
Jesus of Nazareth
                  what man so dead so resurrected
from his breath rush forth the lives of saints in torrents
from the depth of his eyes march forth
transparent armies of confessors virgins martyrs
who after passing through the flames and all the crosses
marching-on return to the depth of his heart
from his mystical fingers sprout highroads to Damascus
from the dust of the earth spring forth the paths which lead to him
his spirit made a habit of coming down as tongues of fire

over the humblest parishes of clerks and woodsmen
it happens every day that men go mad with love for him
with just one parable he makes the dreams of mankind soar
with still another parable he invents the scientific method
a gesture of his gracious hand creates all classic and romantic styles
with just a touch he makes the seven thousand forms of purest
beauty spin
he draws lilies out of acorns
and good from evil by crucifying himself
and burying his divinity in the utmost sinful flesh
and leaping forth from the sepulcher at the speed of light
and leaping forth from the sepulcher in slow motion
expanding in the winds of glory ah such loveliness
who yes who shall tell the story of his deaths and resurrections
against a man like him one cannot strive
the battle he loses is the battle he wins
through invisible proceedings
to him belong forever the tears of the repentant
all the tears of midnight all belong to him
each and every love now works incognito for him
the oldest of his open wounds will never ever heal
those wounds which say I am the way the truth the life
today his resurrected flaming scarlet tunic
flutters in the seven winds yes flutters like an angel
pointing out the true and certain way to paradise
Jesus of Nazareth
what man so dead so
resurrected.

ii

The passion and death and resurrection of Christ
is the only event that ever happened in the history of mankind
the unique event in the history of creation

the only act
what in the end is the making of the solar system

what
if not the first draft of the scene of the passion
what is the birth of the forest green blanketing this planet
if not the seedbed of the timber used to shape the holy cross
what is the formation of the moon

what
if not the luminous effect of the agony in the garden
the olive trees ascended weeping towards the sacred blood
what is the history of Adam and Eve if not the negative of the entire

passion
what is
what is the origin of human language and the discovery of fire
if not the first general rehearsal of the INRI
and that distant clamor called the history of man

what is it then
if not the last breath from the mouth of the crucified
or perhaps the first breath restored to life
what is the third world war if not
Jesus in agony until the end of the world
all the days and all the nights are Good Fridays
speak out the night which does not hold the crucified

the night when his divine blood does not slip away through sewers
the world is a Mass which resembles the world
with the difference that heaven and earth never fail to attend
bent over that chalice of all deaths with infinite curiosity
bent over that veil of Veronica covering the face of God
that's why all the books of the world speak only of the passion
though it may not seem so at first sight
the Encyclopedia Britannica would be an example of that illusion
the Iliad and Odyssey as well
but what is that illusion if not the wound of the open rib
which stares at the author himself like an abyss
the Complete Works of Shakespeare one example
the wind that stirs Veronica's veil another
there are books about the passion that whistle like angels amidst
                                                    the mountains
there are books about the passion in physico-mathematics with
                                                    beautiful equations
which tell how Jesus Christ went mad with love
the Complete Works of Einstein an example
what use would be the speed of light without those wide-open
                                                    agonizing eyes
there are books about the passion in code like the Universal History
                                                    of Toynbee
but what is that illusion if not a thorn from the crown
and who has not heard the wind whistling through the mountains
praying like a dead man the fourteen stations of the via crucis
that wind loves Jesus Christ above all things
and hence it is an angel who goes howling out the entire history of
                                                    the passion
a burnt-out angel is almost as terrifying as an angel all aflame
enough of illusions say the inflamed in every language
let us come now to the point of the history of creation
in the beginning was the Word and the Word was made flesh

once upon a time there was a man called Jesus and
at that time came Jesus speaking in every language
I have come to save all that has been lost.

I. The Final Days

1

He can't recall how long he has been blind
for centuries Bartimaeus has been a dweller of the dark
and at the edge of day he begs the children of the sun for alms
Bartimaeus has no sight but just the fabled ear of midnight
ah with that ear he can hear the voices of the other world
that is how he hears Jesus coming on the timeless day of the
antipodes
and standing at the brink he clamors with the fabled remoteness of
the blind
Jesus son of light have mercy on me
shut up man they rebuke him from the daylight of Jericho
but he cries out over and over again with the fabled voice of suffering
Jesus stops in the middle of the day and calls for him
and that poor son of darkness who lives on simple faith
rushes up to burn his eyelids in the Sun
he lets his cloak fall down like a skin he has outgrown
like a plumage that belongs to the ancient night
what do you want from me asks the eternal light
restore my sight oh Lord restore my sight replies the world
go your way and see your faith has saved you commands the son
of Light
let there be light in the universe as you have believed in light
let there be stars in the night as you have believed in me

and poor Bartimaeus opens his eyes and contemplates
neither the green of the distant hills nor the blue of the star-clustered
sky
but the most luminous face of all creation
there will be time enough tomorrow to look about the cosmos
for now Bartimaeus has centuries to contemplate
the Face that all at once has smiled on him
centuries to live as the first mendicant of everlasting Beauty
to look through the tears of God's love
at the fabled flashing of a thousand suns
at the very face of Jesus Christ the Nazarene.

2

My son my God
whispers King David
through me flowed thy blood swelling like a river
which roared and sinned and lit up kingdoms
impregnated queens and illuminated verbs while marching home
to eternity
my son my God remember me in thy kingdom
in the nights of the full moon I await thee with my powdered bones
by the moon of Bethlehem where I gave birth to thee.

3

Sanhedrin confidential
concerning the psychical state of the Nazarene
we hereby certify that the aforementioned subject
presents an anomaly in his perception of time
as if he were at the same time anterior contemporary and posterior
to the world
as if in every instant he saw the entire history of creation

that man in the affective
incites the absolute love which only a madman can incite
in terms of love that man is a public danger
his self-consciousness is really terrifying
he believes himself to be a species of terrestrial double
with trembling we record here this blasphemy
the terrestrial double of Almighty God
whose name be blessed throughout the centuries
in the external world he mixes up all sorts of different things
like life and death poor and rich sick and sane
Jew and Gentile heaven and earth eternity and time
in short he is completely alienated
and despite his manifest sweetness or because of it
he constitutes a danger to our people
and perhaps to all mankind
as soon as possible he must be taken out of circulation
tomorrow may be too late.

4

By the brim of the well of Sichar
a Samaritan woman sings
five husbands I have had I cannot count my lovers
as many partners of the night as there are midnights
tonight I am alone and I desire no one
because I am a maiden pure close by the waters
in spirit and body virgin to my very nails
give me water to drink the Jew entreated me
it is not that I am lacking in religion
but laugh even the stones through all of Siquem
tonight I am young again and very much in love
I bloom beside the waters like a lily

and with the voice of living water I sing
the sweet song of perpetual virginity.

5

But who say the people is the Son of man
they say so many things the twelve respond
you know how talkative those people are
they write so many things about you lately
they say you are the beheaded and resurrected head of John the Baptist
or the eyes of the prophet Elias embellished by the darkness
they say you are the gentlest of impostors
the man who became God by self-suggestion
he who deceived himself with the most beautiful story ever told
they say you are the first socialist of history
the precursor of Marx in code the first revolutionary
who from the afterlife sends secret orders to the theology of liberation
speaking with the dialectic voice of matter
they say you are the voice which crieth in the desert
with your face hidden by the holy shroud
to avoid the siege of photographers and journalists
among whom you are every day more popular
they say you are the first existentialist
the first ecologist the vegetarian
who along the way converted meat to vegetable
the flocks of Galilee to green pastures
inverting the process of stubborn cattle raising
they say you are the omega point of earthly ecology
they say you are a strictly private problem of conscience
whose public solution would constitute an outrage to our civil liberties
they say you are polymorphous hypothetical parapsychological
the most beautiful myth of the Mediterranean people

a creation of the solar light on those invisible beaches
which every two or three centuries produce a savior
highly acclaimed throughout the world
they say you are the eon that goes between God and the cosmos
the soul of the world disguised as a preacher
the famous missing link of theosophy the Buddha
they say you are the first and loveliest hippie
he who wandered through Galilee with a necklace of wildflowers
followed by a troop of shabby vagabonds that is ourselves
shaking up the bourgeois establishment
shaking up the stock exchanges and the price of gold
they say you are an optical illusion of the masses
which saw you travel through themselves all in blue
they say you are a by-product of the Hebrew tongue
a dream of Saul of Tarsus on his journey to Damascus
the evanescent perfume of an empty flask
in brief concerning you they say so many things
you have compelled the human heart to meditate
behold its delirium to find out who you are
and how the poor heart murmurs in the darkness.

6

But who say ye that I am
you are the light and shadow of Adonai over the earth you are
silence orders Simon who is about to be called Peter
in the name of heaven and earth silence for only I will speak
you are none of those imbecilities
which you have just now gathered from our lips
and whose very enumeration has already overwhelmed us
with all the trash of history
Thou art the Messiah the Son of the living God

the eternal splendor of the Father eternal
God of God Light of Light of one substance with the Father
begotten before the dawn of all the worlds
drawn to earth by the whirlpool of our salvation
by that cross of love which calls you from the depth of your own
absence
you incarnate in the most beloved womb
of the most beautiful of all your creatures
you lineage of David and blood of the authentic Adam
you are the flower of Jesse's tree full-grown
under the direct action of your own Spirit
the light of the patriarchs the dream of the prophets
the alpha and the omega the father of the coming century
you are the point of view of God with regard to the world and the
reverse as well
the only one authorized in both directions
the veiler the unveiler the veil of the face of God
and the reverse the nakedness of the Holy Trinity in our own blind
eyes
you are the purest star of this vale of tears
you are the good shepherd of infinite flocks
that pass through you on their way to greener meadows
whose green is you yourself at the border of God
the one by the mention of whose name Jesus
a thousand demons race forth crying from the human heart
you are he who nonchalantly eats and drinks with sinners and the
only one who truly gives them absolution
and their nourishment sweet to the taste and even sweeter in eternity
you are the most adored image ever painted
by the hand of your death that dreadful hand
and you are the open book wherein the Father writes his own immensity
resorting to your very blood when there be need

you are the sacred heart which makes the sun rise forth out of its
own blood
you are the immensity of each and every love
that which nameless and formless in loving obliterates our very selves
and the Bridegroom of we who blossom as your mystic Bride
you are he who holds the keys to the kingdom of death
he who opens and no one closes he who closes and oh God
you are the one who comes to judge the world in its own fire
you are the eternal life says Simon and he stops
his voice can no longer bear the load of the Father who is in heaven
and after a silence which lasts for centuries over the earth
thou art Peter says Christ and upon this rock
thou shalt see how beautiful I will build my Church
that I shall wed in love.

7

Death comes flying over Bethany
Mary of Bethany breaks an alabaster flask which represents the world
as if it were her own heart she has broken it
and pours the river of perfumed nard over the funereal head of the
Master
the house is overfilled with extreme-unction
ah the perfume of the nard which represents the world which bids
farewell
those who are about to die desire tenderness
Jesus can but does not want to be an exception
Mary dries the adored feet just as that public sinner did
love is identical to itself
Judas estimates the loss to be approximately three hundred denarii
the solution to the food and housing problem of three hundred poor
the poor are I myself in the form of the poor

whom you shall always have with you says Jesus
but in the form of Christ I am unique and so I say farewell
stop calculating me in terms of solutions to the housing problem Judas
don't dare build me churches out of leftovers
I like the alabaster churches
with her own heart this woman has anointed me
yes that may be so but the heart of Judas is the latest model calculator
the Master bathed in nard now bids farewell
the latest model heart begins to calculate
how many dollars or rubles this world will pay for the king of the
                                                  other world who is dying.

8

At midnight Judas thinks
about the three hundred coins 300 about that wasted fortune
ah to squander the perfumes of the poor over the most immaterial head
over the immaterial feet of death
an economic system founded on the power of the invisible
reveals itself for what it is in those gestures of lyrical grandeur
at the expense of the poor of course
Mary that beautiful thief is to be judged by the people themselves
the head of Christ will become visible again with his death on the cross
and the invisible force will return to the real productive base
of the riches we shall always have with us.

9

Matthew the Evangelist is taking note
it must be recorded forever that the fragrance of the perfume of the
                                                                 nard
shares in common with the maiden who pours it over the head of
                                                         the beloved

half a dozen things at least and maybe more
the profound superfluity of everything which is beautiful
the perfect equidistance between reality and dream
the exhalation of the soul on account of love
the inhalation of the soul on account of pain
the power to triumph over eternal death
the natural origin of the woman and the nard
and the property of being two metaphors of the very Church
until death shall them part
and that is why this action is recorded until the hour of
the resurrection of the holy perfumes.

10

And the poor
and the poor are blessed
the blind see and the dead return to life
the lepers shine and glisten like the sun
the rose bushes bear incredible roses
and the Good News is carried to the poor.

11

Confidential report
                for the Sanhedrin
from its intelligence service
                about Jesus
subject surrounded by sorcery from the cradle
witnesses interrogated insist that they saw angels
social class uncertain
                poor and yet
                        blue blood

highly popular among the dead whom he restores to life
large hypnotizing eyes
they say that even the seas which he has calmed become his devotees
he never calls things by their proper name
in his speech there is something intrinsically ambiguous
he preaches in parables with countless meanings
in brief he is a leader who hides behind the mirage of his language
political intentions devastating
as to have himself crowned the emperor of the world through love
                                                 alone
we cannot fathom the meaning of this expression
and from Rome to soar in one incomprehensible leap whose destiny
with horror let it be said and with leave from your Honors
his final destiny is to have himself crowned King
of the Kingdom of heaven forever
                         and ever
                               and ever.

1 2

Edict of the Sanhedrin
order to arrest the Galilean
                        warning
his forms are always changing just like the devil's
his usual face is as handsome as a magician's
he turns water into wine by demagoguery
he cures minor psychosomatic ills
he returns to life psychosomatic dead
he meets all sorts of troublemakers at the close of day
and invites them to his kingdom if they are
publicans thieves or prostitutes
with baneful eyes he looks at us the righteous ones

he insults us with double meaning parables
he calls us vipers or demons or wolves that whistle like the good
shepherd
or excrements that sing like the very angels
he achieves his best results among the lumpen
he masters all the arts and skills of Lucifer
in the darkness he appears as a lamb
his bleating should not deceive a soul
like an angel of light he appears and says
I am the resurrection and the life or I am the light
he appears like a ghost over the waters
he invites his disciples to walk by the moonlight over the waters
by air by sea by land we must be rid forever
of that demon who whistles like the good shepherd.

13

From the centurion Quintus Severus to Pontius Pilate
however strange it may appear oh Procurator
Jesus the Christ is apolitical from birth
just as I say
that agitator is so apolitical it seems he is no Hebrew
he belongs to a species still unknown to us
thus our spies have certified
his teaching in the form of parables refers to a kingdom of the heavens
of the heavens I repeat for your tranquility
and to some other topics of a strictly ethical-religious nature
in terms of seeds and crops of birds and lilies
and a thousand other weeds of land and air
that seem to pose no danger to the government of Caesar
concerning the regime and the nation he observes a silence which
is every bit a program

when questioned on the topics of the day like Caesar's latest tax
reform
he will take a leap abruptly toward the infinite
leaving Herodians and Pharisees open-mouthed and gaping
it is true that some of his disciples speak of kingdom
in the politico-Hebrew sense so well-known to us
yet at once they are reproved like little children by their teacher
the most unbridled political pluralism reigns among his intimates
some belong to the resistance or even to the RRM
whose initials write themselves on the ramparts of the Hebrew night
others are collaborationists or socio-Hebrews or absolutely nothing
but to one after another their master seems to have disclosed such
horizons of a nature yet unknown such bottomless abysses
which are still nameless
that among them the political component is strictly
subordinated
however strange it may appear oh Procurator
excluding the case of Judas Iscariot.

14

Ah let no one say that I did not love Jesus
and who would not have loved those eyes which seemed to be
eternity forever gazing
eternity itself wandering along the shores of Galilee
ah after having seen his early miracles
those fingers which brought healing by remote control
like a madman I roamed about repeating to myself
rejoice oh Zion you shall be the zenith of the universe
rejoice all earth for the liberation of the poor has come
and you Rome tremble and you Judas
and why not
and you Judas get ready you shall be one of his twelve kings

you shall be one of his miraculous fingers
but very soon my disappointments first appeared
everything took on a vaguely spiritual dimension
he healed the servants of centurions as if nothing
he resolved only personal cases
a vast number but solely in so far as they were personal
five thousand hungering mouths satiated in the desert
buy only inasmuch as personal mouths
mere mirages of the gaping mouth of humankind
soon it was seen that his miracles were parables in action
metaphors of the remission of all sins
imprecise allusions to the metaphysical order
whereas the poor
        ye shall have them with you always bah
soon it was seen that he had brought no political upheaval to the
        world
he did not seem aware of such a question
he spoke as if political reality did not exist
those clairvoyant eyes only saw the private heart
blinded by their own light they did not see the world
what does the heart of Judas matter next to the problems of the
        entire world
what does my precious heart matter compared to the enormity of
        social structures
and yet for him my heart remained of primary importance
I was everything for him
his eyes aflame with love became intolerable to me
his eyes saw everything within me
his eyes saw not the people of Israel
it was as if I alone were all of Israel
ah that eternal ambiguity about his messianic condition
I am no King I am and I am not

only in the immaterial sense of the expression King
and then when he declared that he was the Messiah
what tremendous indecision in rising to the occasion
a nice triumphal entrance to Jerusalem was his
a Rabbi dressed for first communion trotting on a donkey's colt
that man's sole desire is to have his throat slit open
Judas get ready for history will absolve you
I don't deny that I possess an economic sense of history
but still I don't consider myself worse than all the others
John who sleeps on the bosom of the Lord how lovely
Peter the rock and James the thunder who sleeps upon his hand
                                                    how lovely

the damned eleven kings of the other world
it will be said that next to them I am vile

                              vile vile
the word vile pursues me from my infancy
I saw it written in the Master's eyes when I was called
the pupils of those Galileans spelled it out
it was multiplied by eleven with the utmost ease
the word vile is my own mirror traveling through the world
well then I know not what it is to be vile
I only know what it is to be Judas
while he so stupidly insists on being a mystical a slaughtered lamb
like a dying man for a long time now he looks at me
I cannot stand his mystical his slaughtered hints
I am Judas and I hate him
                              I hate him
how sweetly sibilates the serpent
                              man I hate him
how important is my name in that underworld
Judas Judas
ah never have I heard a voice so beautiful

since that

        Judas come and follow me

                since that

accursed deception of the other world when I was young.

II. The Last Supper

1

The Red Sea is open say the Egyptians
look what a lovely pathway for anti-Semitic persecutions
wait a minute wait a minute roars the Red Sea
who do you think you are Hebrews and promised people?
wait a minute roar the waves cascading down like oceans
over hordes and hordes of Pharaohs never promised oh what a spectacle
the glory of an entire army drowning in a glass of water
drowning in the glory of Yahve those anti-Semites
who sink to the bottom as the fabled green flash of dying cultures
illuminates the sky.

2

Hear me
the paschal lamb and his death and his blood
and the exodus from Egypt and this promised land
were nothing but a dream about myself
only I am the passage of eternity through itself
I the Lamb who takes away the sins of the world
tomorrow above this world I will be immolated
about me Moses dreamt for me the Red Sea opened
thinking of me the paschal victims perished
the lambs of centuries bleated through my eyes

I am the horizon where the visions burn
I am the first lamb I am the last of all
in this supper I am the feaster and I am the food and I am the drink
when you see my blood upon the cross
know ye that eternity has now begun.

3

Don't go around telling people says Andrew but
though I have never been in Egypt
I have been liberated from the bondage
which for years I suffered in that land of demons
at the same time I confess that in the Red Sea I have never waded
and yet with what supernatural grace
the waters drew apart to let me pass
it's true that I have never been away from Palestine
but I cannot compare a single local journey
with my swift crossing through the ocean beds
escorted by two marvelous high walls of water
though I was born and always lived within the land of Israel
you can't imagine what it meant for me
to cross the threshold of this promised land in flight from Egypt
after passing through interminable deserts
through thousands of troubles before I tread upon my native soil
and once I was settled down in Israel
I thought I would enjoy the pleasures of the paschal passage
look well from whence I came to know that I had not arrived
that this fair paschal land on which I stood in safety
is neither land nor safe nor liberty nor was I ever there
for it was just an image a prophetic dream
of the journey which tonight we are about to undertake
the pilgrimage of freedom will be made through time

ah the future so much harder to pass over than the oceans and the
deserts
we will journey through centuries where we have never been
we will arrive at centuries where we have always dwelt
do not ask me the way because
everywhere the way runs free and
everything is now the way and
the departure and the way and the arrival
is Jesus and is Jesus and is Jesus.

4

The ritual of the four wine cups has finally begun
he first is poured
then Jesus sanctifies the wine and sanctifies the Day
they have brought the bitter herbs together with unleavened bread
and the murky relish to remind the supper guests
of the mud with which their fathers built adobes under the Egyptian
lash
the second glass of wine now makes the rounds
after drinking a few drops of salted water
to commemorate the bitter tears of bondage
the lamb itself arrives with fragrant herbs
the Paschal Lamb of Yahve
this lamb is strange says Judas it tastes of man
this is the last supper of all history
now all recite together the Hallel and the face of Jesus
has turned much darker than the pharaonic mud
verily I say to you that one of you shall soon betray me
the silence of the upper room is dreadful
all the tears of bondage can be heard
the silence asks my God if it were I

and Jesus says it's he who dips his bread into my dish
and offers Judas a sop of bread with all the love
of heaven while all of hell ascends
to take possession of its most beloved son.

5

In this brief aside a forum has been opened in the purest Hebrew style
to designate their ranking in the kingdom on a scale from one to twelve
to whom has it been given the lovely name of Peter argues Peter
I in person will administer the keys to the abyss
yes yes but when we come to intellect and love
says John you surely won't compare yourself to me
my pilgrim eyes already verge upon the end of time
I'll be the historian of eternity itself
perhaps announces Matthew but the history I prepare
offers the matchless advantage of the synoptic and realistic style
it's my faith pronounces Thomas which will cause the world to talk
in either style it will deserve a chapter by itself
Thaddeus then whispers I possess no special title
and therein strictly speaking lies my greatness in the kingdom
did not the Master tell us that the last shall be the
enough enough says Jesus who has suddenly turned visible
who suddenly becomes a slave a parable in action
and picking up a pitcher and a cloth falls down upon his knees
at the feet of
                    his poor
                            apostles twelve.

6

Jesus is the supreme servant of the servants 13
Jesus is washing the 24 dust encrusted feet
those feet of the Orient bear the authentic filth of the Orient
they are not the lovely feet of Adam and Eve in paradise
they are the feet of history
they are the extremities of the fallen animal
that limps and falters sinning through the dust
that sins from foot to head
with the world upside down between his eyelids
at their feet is God washing their feet with his own tears
oh ye who pass by the roadside
tell if there be a flower or an angel or a fly
more humble than our God
the small one who bows before the great is not humble but the opposite
the Eternal has gone down upon his knees
for the feet of Judas he has a mother's hand
oh ye who pass by the roadside
tell if there be any love like that of mother God.

7

Jesus is a dark slave of the first century and
he who wants to follow me must kneel at the feet of the poor
and lick those immense leprosies of reality.

8

It was easy to wash the feet of John
they were the winged feet of love
that loved the water with the unconsciousness of youth
for Peter on the other hand prophetic actions nil

never you to me

the you was the infinite ocean of Reality
the me a lowly leper naked on the shore
but when he realized that he could plunge entire infinite leprous
radiant as the whole sea
the whole power of Christ was needed to restrain him
the feet of Judas let themselves be washed light-years from his heart
the man just simply left his feet discarded in the distance
he abandoned them entirely in that shameful and ridiculous observance
he was not at all impressed
it was as though he had been born to have his cast-off feet aspersed
as though He who had created them had then to wash them clean
on all the Maundy Thursdays of eternity
the hands of Jesus were so tender
Jesus kneeling whispered words of love to the heart which was not there
in God's final hopeless effort to seduce his basest creature
his base creature just stared at the ceiling
and allowed his God to wash his feet dismissed in the distance
on all the Holy Thursdays of eternity.

9

Josemaría Escrivá spent all the washing weeping
his tears flowed down together with the tears of Christ
John Paul the Second was as spotless as an angel
but all the same Christ chose through him to wash
the twentieth century's nauseating feet
preparing by these means the conversion of Russia
oh the heart of the Lord what palpitations.

10

Jesus is a soul about to leave his body
Jesus is a body at the threshold of pure transparency
about to vanish in the love of God
for his body and blood are about to reappear within
this bread within this wine where the concealed and concealer says
take now and eat this is my body
this is my blood of the everlasting covenant that shall be shed upon
the cross
renew this sacrifice in memory of me he says and taking himself in
his own hand
he distributes his communion
and that immolated body now communed has disappeared within
his dozen loves
and once the sacrifice is made oh God that voice of the eternal and
high priest
briefly disappears within the love of God
it is the silent prayer which follows the communion
a dozen inward Christs gaze startled at the outward Christ
the immense communicated ones encompass their own bread
the whole world holds its breath
history is speechless now
only the wind in the wheat fields and the vineyards can be heard
only the whirling of the planets whispers in the air
in his devoured substance Jesus now is trembling
his immolation on the cross begins its pilgrimage world without end
while his body and his blood the victim
with the burden of eleven men has already vanished in the love of
God.

11

Transubstantiation
and the bread oh God lies gently uprooted from itself
and its very real substance on the way to nothingness
in a final flash bequeaths to Christ the precious legacy
of the taste bread the color bread the accidents of bread
miraculously dangling from nothingness itself
because the bread exists no longer and its devoured substance
has given way to the devouring substance of Christ the God
oh God the accidents of bread without the bread
dangling from the void and yet exactly in their place and time
just as lightning reaches its rendezvous
just as a new creation within creation
between Christ and the bread lies the beautiful the timeless the
impossible nothingness
the nothingness which tastes of bread
the nothing with the white and luminescent raiment of the bread
that Christ more naked more beautiful more swiftly than the flash
of light
has wrapped around himself like a luminescent veil
in an instant void of time in a pure and absolute humiliation
and now Christ is the true and the profound and the inexpressible
bread
which enters through the mouth like the sun into a garbage heap
of all the baptized in a state of grace who then devour it
and swiftly as a flash of light are devoured by Jesus Christ their bread.

12

I am the bread of the angels and woe
unto him who receives me in a state of sin as Judas did

I am the death in the mouth I am hell itself
in the innards of that terrifying man.

13

The sacramental Christ of cathedrals or country parishes
beaten down by the rains and by the years
at times inflamed in earthly canticles
and then for days and nights abandoned to a host of angels
to the stony hatred of the demons
oh the nights oh Jesus of the nights
burning in solitude for the sole remembrance of some sleepless man
while millions sleep the sleep of the oppressive earth
while the Father beholds
how the first of all suns is born on earth.

14

Who would have ever thought that I would become a priest
that during the last supper Jesus would ordain me
I the black sheep of Galilee I the nighttime reveller
of the lowest dives of all Cafarnaum
until that day when the Master his eyes aflame with fire
his voice the sound of many waters over those enormous beaches
I didn't know who spoke to me
whether it was the ocean or that half-translucent shadow
what a mad idea no ocean can speak in such a way
the Master fishnet of miraculous catches the Master hands of God
come and follow me he said for thou shall be a fisherman of men
but who would have ever thought that I a priest
three years with him in this world and the other
three years and I a shadow not at all translucent

on certain days I seemed to fly above the heights of Sinai
on other days his parables exploded in my head
but this holy night who would have said it
after the barbarity of his body and blood
nothing less than do this in memory of me I give you power
and no sooner said than done a priest for all eternity
I was trembling I swear it from foot to head
a priest forever after the order of Melquisedec
farewell to the synagogue farewell speaks out the Church
with my hands my newly consecrated hands it says farewell
with tears in the eyes of history I take my leave
of the ancient priesthood of Aaron and the Levites
a star already extinguished in the night of God
for the beard of Aaron I have great respect
and for the ointment trickling down from it according to the psalm
yet Levi and Aaron are now but tears of history
metaphors fulfilled this day by Jesus Christ
a metaphor once fulfilled is blown with the wind
you don't know what awaits you speaks out history to me
the high priesthood of the Christ no wind will ever blow it
it is in fact a portion of eternity
a star that in the night of God will never fade away
because it is already the selfsame dawn of God
modesty apart I am another Christ and Christ himself
I a priest yes sir I an eternal priest
modesty apart I am the dawn of God I
I the blackest sheep of all Cafarnaum.

15

Simon the Zealot goes around examining social sins at dawn
while the personal sins of the world stand in endless lines

waiting for their absolution
go Simon get into your confessional at once
the sermon of the last supper cries out to him
or do you think I gave you those powers superior to the very angels
so that you could go around gaping at imaginary flies in the kingdom
of forget-me-nots?

16

In the small piece of bread which lies upon this table
cosmic matter has been deeply moved
the spirits tremble
we glide away almost eucharistically the rivers say
we open up like sacraments the flowers whisper
what has just happened upon this table
affects me physically says Saturn to its seven rings
and the solar system then repeats the same
we the stars are shining with another light
my speed is still the same yet it is faster says the light
the angels quake in glory
the seven thousand elements of the cosmos have fulfilled their
dream
I don't know how to say it exactly says the cosmos to itself
but I'm under the impression I've been turned into a tabernacle
from here to eternity from here to glory
there is but one short step sing out the wheat-fields.

17

The dying farewell of the Master
is a classic genre
for instance Socrates who existed toward the truth

to the point where truth is almost a religious experience
upon his death his disciples contemplate him as the Idea itself almost
as a god
although he refuses to represent authority
a most improper dogmatism for the explorer of being
he shows them only a possible method of interrogation
his very death in life is a form of interrogation
Buddha the one who dies out of pure wisdom
is a man who has struggled as much or more than Socrates
he alone has understood the illusion of all existence
the cause of universal pain and the method for its extinction
the secret outlet of the river of the metamorphoses
his disciples look on him as the open door of the true Nirvana
although he nobly refuses the pedestal of god
and with a slight movement of his eyelids casts off the lines of illusory
life
while the animals regard him as though hypnotized
next to Socrates or Buddha
how dim appears this cenacle of obscure Hebrews
around a master who will soon overflow with anguish
who will be encircled by the terrors of his heart
but with due respect to the classic dead
oh God what a difference
it would be blasphemous to say that Jesus has discovered truth or
illusion of any sort
blasphemous it would be to say that he has unveiled the enigma of
being
and that upon his death he displays himself in front of his disciples
as an example of that unveiling
Jesus of Nazareth has discovered what the blazes absolutely nothing
he has not plowed heroically through the darkness of the world
in order to attain to a higher law which shines before his agonizing
eyes

he is not a religious or an intellectual personage
his words now more than subtle more than questions to the universe
devote themselves directly to raising the dead
calming the tempests pardoning sins and driving out demons from
the human heart
he is not a soul lit up because he is the Light
he has not pursued the truth because he is the Truth
he is not a hero of the word because he is the Word
he has not discovered even himself
Jesus of Nazareth what the blazes
with the voice of infinite humility simply whispers before he dies
I am the resurrection and the life
I am the light of the world
I Am Who I Am
I Am.

18

I am in the Father and the Father is in me believe me
believe my words and my deeds they speak for themselves
believe the prodigal son when weeping he returns to his father's
embrace
I assure you he's a person worthy of the greatest trust
he is every bit an expert on the Father who abides in me
believe the sicknesses which fled in obedience to my orders
and only appear again in public squares to shout
it's the Son of the Father who sent us away
believe the one sheep lost among the other ninety-nine
who acknowledges me as the only authentic shepherd
its bleating is a public testimony to the Son of God
believe the dead who have been restored to life
they have very interesting things to say concerning me

they are specialists of the love of the Father who is in the Son
believe the restless waves of the Galilean sea
who observe a minute of silence on moonlight nights
which they refer to as The Peace of Christ among ourselves the waves
believe the treasure hidden in the field
its antiquity its surprise discovery its golden splendor
undoubtedly refer to my own person
believe the very demons I expelled
they wander howling through the world and like it or not
they howl out to the seven winds it's He it's He
believe the seed which yields one hundred-fold
that cipher so distinctive of my Father
believe your very sins which I forgave
their absence possesses in your souls the proper form
of the Son who is in the Father of all the heavens.

19

Neither the Jews nor the Romans nor the demons
nor pain nor sin nor death
nor the past or the present or the future
exert any power over his person
it is he who grants the exact degree of power
to Judas and the ropes to oblivion and Caiaphas to the deprecations
to Pilate and to Herod to the nervous system and the night and all
four kingdoms
to the wicked thief to nothingness itself and to his very wounds that
approach him
in an act of perfect liberty he grants them the exact power over himself
to extract from his heart the maximum suffering
which in the use of his perfect liberty he will transform into the
maximum
of love for only love is the exact power of his person.

III. The Agony in the Garden

1

They went out into the night
the immense the sweet the dreadful night
all of the nights of the earth thereafter
do nothing but repeat this very night
hence their unexpected similarity
the full moon of the Passover so in love with the face of Christ
the moon of Nisan peeking over the mountain
for the first time in its life was horrified by the face of Christ
by those lunatic eyes by that dreadful mouth
the eleven were just as horrified as the moon
Jesus' feet went wandering by themselves through the valley of
                                                                    Josaphat
his voice went raving by itself the eleven thought
it said that it would come in person to judge the living and the dead
in this same valley of Josaphat
of course at no specific point in time
oh Lord spoke out the eleven don't get so sad
you'll see tomorrow will be another day
the springtime flowers will be at their best
there's still an age until the end of time the moon suggested
the moon of Nisan so in love
and speaking in this fashion they crossed the brook of Cedron
Jesus' entire face was trembling

36

the moon doubled in the water did not believe what it was seeing
and covered up its eyes with the mountains of Josaphat.

2

At last they reached the place called Gethsemane
the garden of the pitch-black flowers of the spring
in some police station nearby Judas kept his watch
sit ye here said Jesus while I go and pray
my soul is sorrowful and anguished even unto death
watch and pray with me don't leave me all alone
he is like a child frightened by the tremendous night
God fears to be alone in the darkness
Jesus requests three miserable fellows to keep him company
the visions of hell assault him
the sins of the world surround him like a flock
as if they were his own they cast themselves by billions headlong
                                                    into his heart
tonight he takes on all the sins as if his own
tonight original sin wants to meet its new Adam
tonight all the sins of the world want to see themselves
                    at last alone
                              with their own
                                        author.

3

He wants to pay the price of human ransom
stripped of himself this leprous lover
wants to drink up the chalice of himself to the very dregs
meticulously he has given away his divinity
and then no less minutely his humanity

37

what remains is a species of leprous worm
what remains in all his nakedness is Jesus the all-sinning vicar
Jesus the miserable falls to his knees
he is sorrowful and anguished even unto death because of sin
his knees no longer can support such leprosy
Jesus prostrates himself completely on the ground
O Father if it be possible let this cup pass away from me
he is praying beneath the immeasurable weight of all history
the weight of his depravity crushes him against the dust
the Jews only prayed while standing up
this Jew is God and
he prefers the posture of the worm.

4

When a decent man comes to the aid of a certain delinquent
and what decent man does not have at least one delinquent friend
how many precautions does he take to leave it perfectly clear in the
                                                    eyes of society
that he had nothing to do with the affair itself
that he just happened to be passing by with his feet well polished
just see how clean are his hands of compassion
let public opinion acknowledge it sincerely
yet Jesus the immaculate the Saint of saints
bore the weight of all the crimes of human history
taking not the slightest precaution to polish the thorns of his crown
though every friend of his was a delinquent every single one of them
in the eyes of society he left nothing clear at all
rather he entangled himself with his friends in their crime
one thing was clear he was not passing through another's cross by
                                                    chance
for the cross was he himself and he himself the criminal

and that is why he called them my brother and my love and concealed
                                                                them
transgressions and all in his radiant heart he hid them
so that nothing would happen to them he hid them in his conscience
rather it was his friends who were just passing by
through the cross and they said behold the public delinquent
he willed to be sin without taking the slightest precaution in the
                                                    eyes of all society.

5

He caught the flower in the very act of dying
he placed it in his heart to raise it from the dead
he was the leprous flower the most profound
with flower and leprosy and all of him he returned to life.

6

The Son is there in place of all the sinners
all the sins of humankind he suffers as his own
as his own oh Holy God
as his own how impossible abominable heretic-faced
the Son cannot possess as his very own the sins of anyone
yet as his own he suffers them
that as his own is the most insane love of the passion
it's the suit of blood which that loving madman of a Redeemer wears
it's the most secret cabbala of that scandalous Savior
it's the voice of the devil in his heart
it's the insane whistling of the wind through the olive trees
it's the INRI of the agony and the metaphor
that the angels of the lamentation use to mention the fact
every time they ask themselves but how oh God

as his own
take a look at that insane word which has taken flight
no one knows if to heaven or to hell.

7

He is Adam and his original sin has darkened the entire world
and that's why he is sweating blood and ever more blood beneath
                                        the moon of the olive trees
he relished the taste of a luciferian pride
he in person struck with the hand of Cain and struck and struck
the innocent Abel until he beat his brains out
that's why he has to expiate even unto death
he is all the most repugnant creatures of Sodom and Gomorra
he is guilty of everything ever done contra naturam
that's why he must be swept from the face of the earth
he is Marcion he is Manes he is a Gnostic of the darkness
he possesses every evil of the intelligence
and has corrupted Christianity from within
and has disfigured the face of Christ from century to century
that's why he has to perish on the gallows of the cross
he is the worst of all the Borgias and the Medici
he has the eyes of a degenerate artist and the smooth hands of a
                                        poisoner
he is an accursed philosopher and poet far worse than Rimbaud
he cultivated in his soul depravity
by a slow and orderly derangement of all his senses
he went mad after shouting with the voice of Nietzsche
God is dead and I myself have killed him
that's why his Father God has forsaken him
he laid his hands on enormous sums of money at the expense of the
                                        blood of the poor

he invented the law of the jungle and class struggle and the
dictatorship of the proletariat
that's why he must be tried before the courts
it was he who issued the peremptory commands of Hitler and Stalin
it was he who slaughtered millions of innocent victims
whom he himself had rounded up in Auschwitz and Siberia
it was he himself who opened fire right and left and set off time
bombs in the nursery schools
he endowed the twentieth century with the apocalyptic dazzle of
its agony
and constructed nuclear warheads which in cold blood he exploded
in the midst of the teeming and defenseless civilian population
that's why he must be punished on the cross even unto death
it was he who sold his Master for thirty silver coins
he was his own crucifiers
that's why he lies there in the dust of Gethsemane
and in the moonlight sweats a stream of blood
under the fixed justice-seeking and moving eyes of his Father God.

8

Father if it is possible
let this cup pass away from me
it's too horrible to drink one's own self
turned into the cascade of the universal vomit
Father but if those millions of cascading souls need it to be turned
into Christ himself
take pity on the vomited and
Father thy will be done not mine.

9

Ecce homo says God about himself
and the face of Jesus Christ all bathed in blood
appears on the balcony of the universe.

1 0

All the pains of the world were searching for him
the slaps in the face take this take that were coming
from all the ages to smash against his face
all the headaches were summoned forth
the meeting place was underneath the crown of thorns
see you in the wound of the open rib
all the pains in the heart exclaimed to one another
if we fail to find his heart we're absolutely lost
without his heart we will never be pains
without his conscience we will never be anything at all
exclaimed to one another all the ailments
of the stomach bones and skin
of the respiratory and neurovegetative systems
without his own system we will never be possible
in the garden is the man they said to one another
he is as strong as death but we will hurt him all the more
for some good reason we are the first-born sons of sin
the night of the prostrate man is only now beginning
we have millennia ahead of us to torture him
the neuroses of the world were seeking him out
in their characteristic tortuous fashion
the anguish of the twentieth century was totally his
without him there will be no twentieth century the anguish said
the psychoses of the world were seeking him out
with their characteristic lucidity

the insomnias of centuries kept watch over him
ah how many centuries did he spend without sleep
he was tortured in every prison cell
he was raped abused and strangled
in all the forests of nocturnal terror
in every corner of Babylonia
he woke up dying from hunger dying of cold
all the civil wars sundered him in two
all the world wars left him devastated
they could not think of anything else to do with him
he was every innocent victim
he was every guilty victim
he was the childless parents he was the abandoned wife
he was every prisoner and every gendarme
the concentration camps overflowed with him and
those endless lines on their way to nowhere were him behind himself
ecce homo serenely undergoing martyrdom
from one single instant of his unshaken courage
every martyr of history is born.

11

The pains of the world have an excellent memory
they never forget that once they were Jesus
they tug at the soul that endures them
saying
      I am Jesus
               your redeemer of last night
help me to redeem the world with thy very self
only three more nights and then
                    resurrection.

12

Master speaks out Peter
I dreamt that you were dying in the night of the garden
the demons were watching over your pallid agony
between blood and stench your kingdom was dying out
I awoke on the air of dread and I felt
your eyes inside of mine while sin and death
were gazing at me from the depth of my dream
sin and death were you yourself.

13

And all the slaps of history
must land in his face
were it not for that sweet face
the slaps of history would remain immobile
and we would never know we have a face.

14

Jesus passed through that scoria as well
endogenous exogenous depression
the anguish of insomnia in the dark
all that scoria from this night on shall be
for the poor fellow
trembling amidst the humid olive trees
the divine path that leads him on to glory.

15

Father if it is possible
let pass from me into the infinite

the invasion of Poland by the Nazis
the invasion of Prague Budapest Warsaw by Russian tanks
the desolation of Vietnam by American bombs
the disappearance of Paris in the mirrors of its brothels
the disintegration of Jerusalem by celestial hosts
remember that I am millions upon millions of crazed inhabitants
like drops of blood which roll over the immensity
of my earthen face oh Father if it is possible
let this cup of myself pass away from me.

16

An angel was sent from heaven to bring him comfort
but how does one comfort my Adonai my Kyrios
thought the angel with the speed of thought when he encountered
passing through the foliage of Gethsemane
the moonlit bleeding face of Jesus Christ
a phantom dreadful even for an angel
he needed to emit every lumen of his light
to recognize in That Thing the deity eternal
he did not weep for angels never weep
he did not die for angels never die
but trembling like a flame for it is true
that angels shudder like the purest fire
from the depth of his pure spirit he brought forth trembling
a host from heaven a luminous wafer
and he placed it in the half-open mouth of his God
in the bleeding jaws of his Adonai he placed it
and immediately like a lightning he disappeared
like a lightning he wandered through the ether
he could not locate heaven because he was out of his mind
and when finally he recovered the glory

which he had given up as lost forever
he engulfed himself completely in the Face shining up above
which down below was fading like a dying dog.

17

Those drops of blood floating over the garden
trickle down oh God over the garden as if God Himself
were in his heights
agonizing.

18

The unborn children of contraception appear before him weeping
                                                    out their hearts
they beg him for his very flesh in order to be born
Jesus I love you they tell him with their eyes made out of nothing
Jesus already pure imaginary flesh
sweats oceans of his precious blood that will never redeem
those weeping non-existent children who appear at midnight
those wet pale beings who disappear within their childless mother.

19

His knees his hands oh how they tremble
how his nerves are vibrating in the outside air
like a castaway he walks in the outside world
he approaches his three disciples standing watch
the three lookouts of the world's redemption
the castaway survives out of sheer courage
by power of pure love he walks about in agony
he begs his three lookouts for consolation

he would like to rest his bloodstained head
against the breast of John against the rock of Peter
even the simple glance of James would be sufficient
but all in vain the three are overcome with sleep
that modest paradise in black and white
that sanctuary which nature denies to no one
is denied only to Jesus Christ and Judas
the three watchmen awake but do not recognize the castaway
watch with me but one sole hour for the love of God
it's he it's he sustained by the grace of pure angels
it's he who survives by the miracle of his courage
it's he who has not obtained even the alms he was begging for
but all in vain he has no comforter
the dust of the ground is his only brother.

20

The apostles may sleep but the mother keeps watch
the mother is in agony until the end of time
the mother of Jesus like the full moon of Nisan
illuminates the valley of Josaphat
she extends her pure almost translucent hands
towards the garden which calls her like her blood
for it's blood of her blood the blood of God
that she cleanses from the distance with her hands
of light with so much love that Jesus feels them
just as if they were touching his dark face
ah what relief this sole earthly comfort
what tenderness from heaven comforts his dark face
as if nothing had happened in those three long years
as if nothing at all in those last thirty-three
Jesus is crying with love just like a child

because heaven and earth have abandoned him
but the leprous the abandoned the offspring
has a mother and his mother is the entire love
of heaven and earth and she is watching over him
and she is washing his face all bathed in blood
by remote control like the light itself
as in Bethlehem then his very blood
the leper of God the everlasting man
has a mother and his mother is all the comfort
of the kingdom of this world the sweet kingdom
because Mary exists upon the dark earth
and God in his very agony whispers oh mother
do not abandon me mother oh my mother.

2 1

Jesus now all powerful awakens them
get up let's get going the hour has arrived
here comes the sleepless kiss which will betray me
wherefore art thou come my friend my beloved Judas
Judas my beloved Judas thou with one sole kiss
it's astonishing what a single kiss can do
Judas the beloved thorn the most select
the most painful thorn of all the passion.

2 2

The mystical Lamb hovers on the heights of Mount Zion
and with him the one hundred and forty-four thousand who bear
his name
and the name of the Father inscribed on the forehead
are singing with the voice of countless waters

a new canticle which no one at all can sing
except the one hundred and forty-four thousand robed in scarlet
tunics
and their song goes like this we are the blessed
converted only and solely by the agony in the garden
we are the stone-hearted saints
we are the stones converted into tears
we were broken up and liquified we cried exclusively
when we saw God sad falling on his knees
moaning and sweating with the sweat of blood forsaken
we were converted only in the name of anguish
we are the one hundred and forty-four anguishes of God
the first-born of his courage in the fullness of his agony
not even the cross in person could free us from the cross itself
only the pass away from me this cup oh Father could convert us
into the blessed who sing eternally like tears
the hosanna of fear the ecce homo
of the courage of Christ the Alleluia
of the panic of God in Gethsemane.

IV. The Jewish Trial

1

Where are your magic arts then Son of God
they seem to be powerless against these ropes
ah there's nothing like some sturdy ropes
for the Son of God in his moonlight outings
giddap giddap my God
reaching the brook of Cedron they fling him down
they hurl him from the bridge for your thirst oh Son of God
verily the Psalm 110 must be fulfilled
my Lord shall drink of the brook on the way
the escort instead protests but what a shame
that the Psalm 91 is not made use of in this case
the angels shall bear thee up in their hands
lest thou dash thy foot against a stone
but what a lazy angel our Messiah has
imagine falling into the river with his guardian angel
giddap giddap my love another plunge
it'll do you good to drink moon water for your magic tricks
giddap you'll need all your legions of angels to reach the last
judgment alive.

2

The night of the encircling valleys is brimming over
with apostles hidden in the foliage
the night of Pontius Pilate is all a bustle
Claudia sleeps beside him but tosses in her dreams
she speaks and cries and moves within her nightmares
the night of the outskirts of Ophel is but one long lamentation
what will become of us if they take away the sacred heart
the blind see him passing by with the light he himself bestowed on
them
the same voices he bestowed upon the dumb acclaim him now
the night of Annas' palace is flooded with phosphorescence
the prince of this world dances in the blaze of their torches
thousands of lambs are bleating in the outskirts of Jerusalem
the paschal victims bellow at night as if they knew
the moon is threatening and full of signs
the moon is all stirred up and trembling as if it knew.

3

I request the floor says Nicodemus
this trial is null and void according to the Scriptures
regarding its nullity I refer you to Leviticus 19
our law requires the light of day for every trial
you well know how the darkness deforms the perception of the law
and in truth this night is blacker than the very mouth of hell
regarding the life of the Galilean I refer you to the light of day
of the witnesses out of shame I hold my tongue
of the blows which the Galilean has received for remaining silent
I prefer to remain silent out of shame
here the sentence has come before the trial
furthermore

to proclaim oneself Messiah constitutes no crime for if it were
then the Messiah would carry to the tomb the secret of his identity
which would nullify the historical rationale of Israel
if this man is not the Messiah we are wasting our time
he will be forgotten or remembered only to be pointed out with a
finger
behold the madman who claimed to be Messiah
look at him there sitting in the ashes and the dust covered with flies
with rats scurrying all about his naked feet
while his imposturing eyes stray off into the infinite
but if the Galilean be the true Messiah
silence venerable elders I have the floor
if he be the Christ you will find yourselves one day with the absolute
horror
of having waged war against God in person
silence please let me finish speaking
and in that case it will be our children who will be pointed out by
the finger of the centuries
behold the wandering crucifier turned into ashes and dust of his
own feet
it will be their eyes which will stray off into the infinite
they themselves will be the swarm of flies which buzz about the
holy dreadful Face
and they themselves will be the naked rats between the feet of the
divine Galilean Judge
as for me before I turn to dust I take my leave
to save my soul in the presence of Jesus.

4

Caiaphas exasperated
sees the way of the cross receding toward the horizon
sees his own eyes receding into the infinite

enraged and eyeless he descends the stairs
takes a close look at Jesus scrutinizes almost touches him
as if he were God

                         yes how he stares at him
for an instant it seems as if Israel were about to see God
and to his face into his very eyes he vociferates
I adjure thee by the living God that thou tell us whether thou be the
                                       Christ the Son of God
the Christ shall be the most willful victim of history
thou sayest it replies the Christ and furthermore I say unto you
ye shall see the Son of man coming in the clouds of heaven seated
                                     on the right hand of Power
and the Christ sees himself coming in his splendor
and hell sees itself through the open sky
and hell hurls its furies on the Sanhedrin
Caiaphas returns to himself from out of the infinite
and rends his clothes and through his open clothes
the nothingness is seen
and he roars he has spoken blasphemy you yourselves have heard it
yes an insignificant Galilean with his face all smeared with blood
                                        and spittle
has claimed to be the Messiah and the Son of God
that is why all abysses are roaring
he is guilty of death he has spoken blasphemy and he must die
at last at last hell knows now where it stands
Caiaphas sees the way of the cross approaching on the horizon
he no longer cares to have lost his eyes in the infinite
he is only a gaping mouth of hell who says
with a cold and steady voice to his men at arms
I deliver to you this King this God
render unto him the honors he deserves
and in your homage do not skimp the feces.

5

The Sanhedrin police force greets him with thumps
oh how the Son of man has fallen from the clouds of mighty Power
to the level of mortals what a divine smack
now they have crowned him with straw from the latrines
behold the son of David wearing the crown of the King his father
now they have dumped fresh excrement upon his head
behold the anointed of God in the gardens of paradise
now they stuff his mouth with filth
this is the King who offers his son a wedding feast
now they blindfold his eyes and smite him
prophesy who is it that caressed you
now we will carry you to the bridal bed of the divine spouse
now they have drenched him with a pail of piss
this is your precious unction your perfume of the nard
it could have been sold for three hundred denarii
but no because your head deserves the best
only liquid and solid honors of optimum quality
you will not be with us always precious paschal lamb
the paschal Lamb of God walks slowly to his cell
while from the darkness of his septic face
burst lightning bolts of love for all his foes
beneath the crap the urine and the mud
His Highness shines unblemished in the night.

6

They can do with him whatever they feel like doing though it is clear
that he's the one who controls all events from the inner sanctum of
his sacred heart
that his love writes the story of his passion
that his blood writes itself from the inner sanctum of his Father God.

7

The portress said to Peter art not thou disciple of the Galilean
I can see it in your face you can't deny it I'm a first-rate physiognomist
woman what on earth is it you're saying
he stood up petrified and walked around in circles
the rooster crowed but Peter did not hear it
never did he have such great a need for that accursed fire
and now again a constable most surely you're a disciple of
me disciple oh what rubbish I'm wholly autodidactic
the walking once again the fire once again the aged crone
knock it off you're the Nazarene's disciple
your Galilean accent gives you away
out of his wits Peter appealed to the angel of Yahve
may he tear the eyes out of my face if these eyes of mine
have ever seen from close that fellow Jesus
and taking advantage of a distraction of the guards he stole away
in the precise instant that the rooster crowed a second time
and Jesus drubbed was led into his prison
in that precise instant Jesus looked at him
with his clear eyes through the darkness of his septic face
Peter fulminated by the tenderness of that look
went forth into the immense night and burst out crying
the look of Jesus was gentle and in spirit meek
a gentle look without the least reproach
ah how dreadful such a gentle look can be
tenderness with what violence can it punish
with what love more painful than hell Jesus gazed at him
Peter's icy chill became a fire as from hell
his fear became the purest pain of love
now would he cry out to the whole world that he was the disciple
of the holiest and loveliest Master ever known
of the most adorable humiliated God

now would he cry out to the universe that he was the filthiest of all traitors
Peter suffered more than if he had no eyes
than if the angel of Yahve had emptied them completely
and went forth into the vast night of his blinded eyes
like a child in a panic blind with love
and cried with his whole being as if he had no eyes
and cried bitterly with his autodidactic eyes.

8

Again and again his very ministers deny him
in the temples of Caiaphas where they have only changed
the midnight roosters for artificial flowers.

9

Friday dawns
Jesus does not wake up because he has not slept
in his cell he has kept watch over the poor beloved universe
the Good Friday of his passion has arrived
on this new day the poor beloved universe is represented
by a ray of tremulous light which penetrates
and greets the paschal lamb trembling in each of his blood-red wounds
Jesus stretches out his captive hands towards the light
and tenderly returns its greeting
Jesus gently thanks his Father for this day
he is giving thanks with his lacerated lips
that ray has come to him just like the judge who comes
to see the convict in his cell for reconciliation
and Jesus at the dawn of the day of his immolation
has comforted the ray has kissed it and bids it now farewell
like a let there be light for the newborn world.

10

The trial next morning is a mere formality
Israel is ruled by jurists not by poets
we must observe the letter of the law which kills
we must kill in the full light of day
full speed ahead Caiaphas asks the questions of last night
sleepily yawning impatient tell us once again
for the letter which kills in the daylight
I adjure thee by the living God whether thou be Christ et cetera
he has spoken blasphemy et cetera but unhappily
accursed be the eagles of the power of Caesar
there's no letter which can kill if Tiberius Caesar
does not kill with his own Roman law
venerable elders says Caiaphas
we'll have to give our indictment dammit
a political flavor
humiliating I concede but indispensable
if we speak of blasphemy before uncircumcised ears
Pilate will tell us your theologies are your own affair
what can that devil know of theology
we'll have to charge the accused of sedition against Caesar our
blessed overlord
and that this subversive element forbids payment of the tribute
yes the economic touch wouldn't hurt
that he forbids rendering unto Caesar that which is Caesar's
yes the political touch is a mere formality
Rome is governed by jurists not by poets
we must observe the letter of the law which kills
we must kill on the full cross of day
in keeping with the strictest Roman law
dammit.

1 1

At all costs he must confess his criminal designs against Tiberius Caesar
the special services subject him now to cosmic rays
shock immersion in the excrement sham crucifixions
now the accused is nothing but a gray phosphorescence who appears
through the windows
of the cell of confessions with a whisper
I confess that I am the Son of God.

1 2

Judas wandered all over that Last Night
through the valley of Hinnom wandered thirty desperate coins
the light of hell burned brightly in the courtroom of Caiaphas
there he ascertained the smallest detail of the trial
all over the Last Night he fled from heaven he fled from hell
from his shadow he escaped from his body from his haunted soul
he fled from God he fled from man from being and from nothingness
he fled
and in the midst of nothingness he met with men at dawn
who rose out of themselves and looked at him and whispered to one
another you know
he will suffer under Pontius Pilate and will be crucified
killed and buried yes he bears the burden of infinite sorrows
they whispered and looked at Judas strangely and disappeared
making the sign of the cross in the air of their transparency
until once more in the streets of nothingness at dawn
other men appeared even more translucent eyeless now
who spoke like the wind through Judas and whistled you know
for thirty shekels of silver his beloved disciple sold him
this early morning they speak of nothing else in hell
through the streets of nothingness raced Judas like the wind

while Jesus suffered for him more than for the whole creation
and in vain he dreamt of Judas crying at his own feet
in vain he dreamt of pardoning his leprous love
for Judas repentant but desperate was fleeing
beneath the weight of thirty coins as heavy as a cross
transformed into a single kiss with neither hands nor feet he ran
through the streets of nothingness until he reached the temple
which rose there darkly and abruptly in the midst of nothingness
the mouth of the kiss raced in shouting to the priests
who scorned the commercial ventures of that turbulent wind
Judas in a fury hurled into the sanctuary all thirty shekels
and came racing out into the nothingness through the garbage dump
of Hinnom
while the devil followed close upon his heels through the valley of
damnation
whispering like the wind into his ear verses from the Holy Scripture
Cain where is thy brother Abel his blood is calling me
at the sight of the garden of olives trembling he heard
the beloved voice the hateful voice oh Judas wherefore have you come
with a single kiss oh Judas you betray the Son of man
the heart-rending voice of Jesus Judas my love oh my beloved
was inaudible for only the ancient voice of the Scriptures could be
heard
piously murmured by the devil himself Judas oh Judas
you have clothed yourself with curses like a vestment
oh loathsome creature with our own hand go redeem your repugnance
execute the supreme act of justice toward you yourself
oh Judas dispenser of justice oh leprous kiss offer your lips
to the kiss of death a thousand times deserved oh Judas
this garbage dump of damnation is your greatest chance
at this very moment the flesh you sold is being flogged
apply the law of God to yourself then for yourself you will be God

oh Judas your justice is grand now be done with yourself
be done with the carrion of the universe behold there stands
the tree of justice in the depths of the ravine
look how it stretches out its arms towards your neck how it calls you
look how your waistband weeps for your beloved neck
and the band now binds his neck to the tree of the full moon
and the body vomits out its viscera like the labor pains of hell
your justice is great oh Judas you who hang from the full moon
gently rocked by the wind in the air of the hollow night
Judas the dispenser of justice is no more and his strangulated ears
can hear no longer the heart-rending cry of Jesus
Judas my love oh my beloved that strays off into the infinite
like the chosen the most painful thorn of all the passion.

V. The Roman Trial

1

SPQR
the insignia of Roman power shine at dawn
Pontius Pilate dedicates an imperial yawn to Annas and Caiaphas
I'm not complaining you know the Roman is an early riser
that's the whole secret if you want to dominate the world
early to rise
but the break of day
        so pure
                is not the moment for
yes I realize it's a case of life or death
it's clear from his appearance
he seems to be none other than your fabled paschal Lamb
early in the day you begin to skin him
move in closer to hear what
it's true I seem to have forgotten your peculiar laws
you're contaminated by a praetorium yet not by a beheading
well you know a little more blood won't rob me of my sleep
I'm a Roman a son of my times what do you expect
but what terror from the heavens hangs over this disfigured man
that you should go on nailing him to the cross?
aha so he's a public threat to Caesar
so he tries to destabilize our Ceasar by remote control from Jericho
I'm greatly pleased with your concern for Caesar's instability

aha so this man heals the sickly on the Sabbath
couldn't he cure me of my blasted rheumatism
nothing less than on the Sabbath what a horror
it's clear that you are healthy
so he calls himself the luminous Messiah of the promises
even your king even God
allow me please a fourth or fifth imperial yawn
it's the hopeless tedium of life in the Middle East
so full of gods

        I supposed as much.

2

King of the Jews approach
royal blood has always fascinated me
you at least should have no fear of contamination
so then you're king of this great people
you can tell me everything in strictest confidence
it will all remain a secret of the hearings
so then your kingdom is not of this world
so my authority derives from your Father

        from the other world
this king is mad but his madness looks upon me from the other world
with the eyes of the logos can any doubt remain
this king speaks in dreams but no doubt his dreams speak dreadfully

        in earnest
and even more dreadfully his dreams stay silent
his silence soon will question me about my crimes
please I'm the judge so break your silence tell me who you are
he who belongs to the truth you said?
we're not getting anywhere with this man
he is leading me unto personal grounds

by Jupiter unto the grounds of my own conscience
the truth oh yes the truth
                    and what is truth?
at least in the external forum I can notice something in the distance
one of those wandering philosophers who renounce the temporal
he has a touch of those illuminated Grecians
of those incorporeal Greeks who still go wandering about the Empire
selling their abstractions as if they were bread
the truth and what is truth
this king says nothing but his silence is about to proclaim
that the truth is he is he is he
nobody has ever spoken like him solely through his eyes
the truth the other world I am the truth
enough of metaphysics now enough of mysticism!
I'm no Greek mystic of the golden age
I'm not the greatest Hellenic philosopher who ever lived
I'm not a poet I'm a politician
that's why I'm here to govern this people so wrapped up in the other
                                              world
this man is innocent though he fails to aid his case before the law
say a word to me oh Jewish king your silence
is more appalling than your other world
elders of Israel approach
in this man I find no roman fault at all
a subversive from Nazareth
                    Galilean did you say?
then take him off to Herod and I
oh my gods what a relief his wandering silence
is leaving now
it's gone.

3

I congratulate myself on this unexpected meeting
even the Galilean stones are raving about your miracles
I thought you were the resurrected head of John the Baptist
with great relief for my principles now I see
that you're a conjurer from birth completely on your own
of course we have a matter to be settled
you have called me vixen in front of half the world
for calling me mismarried John the Baptist lost his famous head
but I'm the first one to admit that adjectives play tricks on mystic
souls
among whom I dare include myself
let's bury the hatchet then
it's true indeed that my distinguished father may he rest in peace
shed the blood of thousands of new-born infants
reasons of state you understand
in search of your blood which turned invisible
even then your supernatural arts
delivered you from a premature death
believe me I'm the first one to rejoice
Galilean stop staring into empty space
listen to me
although I'm not out of this world I too have devoted myself to
wisdom
despite the burdens of my exalted office
I know a thing or two of occult forces
we two are esoteric intellectuals
Galilean say a word to me
I can't stand your silence of the beyond
Galilean to the point
occult forces have placed you in my hands
proving the relative nature of your power

and the strength of mine
if you perform a miracle for me I'll set you free
I don't ask you for the resurrection of the dead or the taming of the
oceans
I realize the sublime is bound to its own moment
some simple transmutation of the elements will do
dedicate to me some tiny miracle of less importance
with its corresponding method to be sure
if not I'll hand you back to Pilate disguised as a king
even the stones will mock the purple of your tattered rags
silence
silence from the kingdom come of Jesus
that silence annihilates everything
Herod exists no longer
now his court fades away in the transparency
his esoteric voice becomes a murmur
that is lost at the bottom of the nothingness.

4

It is not difficult to talk with Jesus
he made no fuss about the ones he talked with
he required no certificate of good behavior
he required no certificate of birth
he even spoke with the dead if necessary
for instance when he gave them orders to return to life
children angels and adulterers all conversed with him
up to the very end he spoke with Judas
never did he disdain to talk with demons
he treated lunatics with utmost courtesy
he bestowed his full attention on each and every sinner
including harlots when required

with Caiaphas that Lucifer he exchanged tremendous words
he asked and he responded to the sceptic Pilate
only Herod the esoteric worldly miracle-faking sensual lustful
intellectual
received from Jesus the most absolute silence
it is doubtful whether Jesus even looked at him
it is likely that looking at the personage
he saw nothing but the glint of his empty throne
only for the esoteric worldly intellectual et cetera
Jesus is a total silence of the afterworld.

5

The truth and what is truth
who would have ever fancied Pontius Pilate
wrapped up in metaphysics and theology
when even poetry makes my head spin round
let's begin with the most elemental
I can't discern the nature of myself
a haunted soul a victor
a real bastard and yet a son of heaven
a nephew of some obscure demon
an insect who directs his antennae towards the infinite receiving
no reply
a bit of matter programmed by itself
a fallen spirit a badly programmed angel
a flower in evolution or an ancient sun
that flickers out together with the Roman Empire
a greedy beast the center of the world a breath
a tunic in the wind a dream a useless passion
maybe we are but the imagination of Caesar
clearly we know nothing beyond empirical and sensory experience

who is this who speaks to me as if he were
the truth in person or the eyes of the other world
had I let him answer me
he would have said I am the Truth with a capital T
in his eyes I read the capital letter
and after all what practical importance can there be
if someone claims to be Jove's very double
when truth is something neutral illusory indifferent
a mere hallucination of the human language
we have much more pressing business than the metaphysical
for example what is to be done about this king
should we crown him with flowers or with thorns
the truth and what is truth
Pilate is the truth and that is that
I like this teaching of epistemology
Pilate is the truth and Pilate is the lie
I am the truth of the world and its greatest error
Pilate back to your judicial business
what relief here comes Claudia from this world
the hour of philosophy has ended.

6

I dreamt all night about the Galilean
what horror and what sweetness those human those divine eyes
when I awoke I saw them in the praetorium they looked at me as
                                                    in my dream
they are drenched in blood yet identical to themselves
Pilate if you should ever harm those eyes of heaven
not even in your dreams
not even in your dreams will you see again on earth the eyes of your
                                                    beloved Claudia.

7

I know his gaze far better than does Claudia
if only what I saw within his eyes were but a dream
from what world comes this man in case he is a man
an offspring of my gods in transit through the world
or perhaps a luminous scion of the Hebrew heaven
comparative religion is not my strong point
it seems that it's impossible to do without theology
oh Caesar oh my gods shed some theological light on me
let's see now what the forms of the clouds have to say
they say nothing so I feared
if my gods take offense they could harm me on the morrow
the very likelihood requires me to crucify him
but if the future should belong to those long-term eyes
I who have always held the winning card oh my gods
oh my gods whoever you are in the name of heaven tell me
the truth and what is truth.

8

Crucify him roars the public square
but he is meek and humble he is
crucify him right away
but he has converted barbarian nations has turned beasts into
                                                    Gothic saints has
crown him with a crown of thorns
has created such a plethora of beauty has put a bit of order into
                                                    universal history has
nail him to the cross
but he has opened the doors of eternity he is God incarnate he has
in the name of God crucify him right away
his blood be upon us and on our children!

9

The lashes now are stained with royalty's symbolic color
the culprit is contorted into shapes of various animals
the most suitable and biblical image is the worm
though his groans are reminiscent of the lamb
the overall effect is stereophonic
the groaning of the victim the roaring of the people the hissing of
                                the lashes the moaning of the victim
the shouting of the floggers then a silence gone astray
and in the background all the time the bleating of the paschal lambs
three times the cycle is repeated
when the physical strength of the floggers drains away
their replacements arrive with new energy with a spirit of emulation
new scourges tipped with virgin prongs of iron
the body now is scarred with blotches of diverse tonalities
among which may be mentioned
the bluish the purest red the almost black with whitish fringes
the blood spurts from the lamb-like worm a meter and a half at least
then comes a screaming in crescendo kill him
                                wipe him from the earth
the second pair exhausted yields its place to a third
which lacking now a target to be flogged
inverts the victim's body
Jesus now is face to face with his flagellators if one can call it face
the sight of unbruised flesh inflames them
when all his skin is red or black or blue or in between
the worm-like lamb is loosened from the pillar
and falls unconscious in the puddle of his blood
during all three cycles angels weep around Jesus
their tears convey his groanings to the Father
his prayer and his moaning and the dead dog silence
of the King robed in his new and naked purple mantle

his puddle screams to the Father the fathomless unconscious love of
the Savior of the world by love alone.

10

Long live the hair-shirt and the fasting and the scourges
and every form of physical or spiritual penitence
for they ascend to God with the very force of God's love
and with the strength of God's love they make a Christ out of
the gentle body fastened to the pillar.

11

Some ingenious soldiers
approach a heap of firewood for hell
wait until we fashion a crown for our king
thorns turned inwards if you please
the thorns are made from buckthorn rhamnus spina Christi
the length of a hand the width of a bludgeon
a species banned from paradise with Adam
and they thrust the barbed helmet on his head
now the scepter in his hand a whistling reed
next comes the coronation ceremony
ah the old merry customs of the legionnaires
and the virile traditions of the sons of Mars
ah the regal profundity of carnivals
then ave Caesar bows and genuflections
urine and spittle and beatings once again
what more do you want your majesty king of the other world
the courtiers make merry with the regal blood
yes the prophetic blood amuses them no end
while the chorus from the public square howls out

in polyphony a cappela
crucify him
              kill him once and for all.

1 2

Prophesy oh king of the Jews
who is it who smote thee oh King of the Etruscans
prophesy oh prophet prophesy oh blind man's buff
from whose gut has this excrement oozed out
king of the rain and king of archipelagos
oh haunted prince who is it who covered you with spit
oh King of thorns who crowned you
with this headdress of eternity
when are you taking flight oh monarch of yourself
blind man's buff oh when will you ascend
to that kingdom you enjoy in the other world.

1 3

And the Word was made flesh
flesh of the butcher's shop of Auschwitz wholesale Jewish flesh
flesh of the primary schools of Gulag of the asylums flesh
transformed into Communist fat beneath the snow flesh
transformed into the Church of silence of the archipelagos
flesh of the slaughterhouse of the Folies Bergère see display in the
                                                             window
flesh nights of Paris deluxe for sale at retail only
flesh of the suicides that appear in the early light
floating face downward on the rivers of the capitals
flesh of aborted fetus the best quality for cosmetics
flesh of every martyr flesh of Jesus who dies

in the systematic persecutions of the great empires
flesh of genetic engineering of the sorrowful spirits
secret flesh of the KGB transformed into secret information
naked flesh of the CIA published on the front page naked
flesh of Jack the Ripper and his prostituted victims
flesh of Herod in heat flesh of the Baptist beheaded
by the flesh of Salome trembling beneath her seven veils
flesh in the claws of cancer black pest flesh and flesh of snow-white
                                                                    leprosy
flesh with a toothache flesh of mental illness
flesh disintegrated by atomic radiation and vanished into nothingness
dog-flesh cannon-fodder flesh and flesh of the flagellation
solar translucent flesh self-expanding within the immensity of God.

VI. The Via Crucis

1

The Way of the Cross is exactly nine hundred meters long
those nine hundred meters are the longest in all creation
the theory of relativity is struck dumb by that distance
the cross weighs exactly 154 pounds
those 154 pounds are the heaviest of all the universe
our galaxy gravitates entirely around that cross
the force with which Jesus embraced it and carried it up to Calvary
cannot be given physical expression it is the immensity of God's love
there is neither solar
                         nor cosmic calendar
                                        which can measure
the time Jesus needed to carry out that infinite task
when time has blotted out all the ways of this poor world
Jesus will still be climbing with the cross on his shoulders.

2

The man who bears the weight of all our history
is in a very poor historical condition
he can barely drag along the weight of his own spirit
sleepless drained of blood consumed dehydrated
his body is a desert a roaming mirage all the way up
the visibility of the way is bad

his eyes are veiled by blood and blinding spit
his right arm lovingly presses the cross against his shoulder
like a conditioned reflex of the world's Redeemer
the last enamored effort that flows from his own mirage
his left hand like an old lady on a stairway
lifts the vesture which is tripping up his feet
his stumblings are humiliating ridiculous pathetic
the escort bursts out laughing showing him hammers nails and rope
up above we'll hold the party you'll see how high we can exalt you
they say the view is perfect from the cross of Christ
the lips of Christ are praying for his crucifiers
as if they were the apple of his blinded eyes his heart goes loving
the people who insult him from the rooftops and the windows
and the children who scatter stones beneath his lacerated feet
suffer the little children to come unto me.

3

Christ's encounter with his mother
the glances they exchanged in one brief second
is the episode of the passion which has consumed myriads of angels
in its blazing fire
it's the most secretive communication ever held between this world
and the other
it's the theology of history in a transparent state
it's the sanctity of suffering which looked at itself in the mirror and
found itself the same
it's the most painful love at first sight which God has ever experienced
it's the second that has endured the most centuries of transfixion
it's the most comprehensive look that God has ever cast upon the world
that God has bequeathed to the world as the most perfect relic of
his own eyes
and that the Holy Mother Church preserves intact within its heart.

4

The king of the Jews has stumbled once again
his body is a confused anecdote beneath the cross
the worst of all is that someone tripped him up on purpose
let's see now who was the witty fellow who tripped him up let's see
the clever one who made him fall who made God trip and stumble
it is I in person you yourself and no one else
no more dissembling man for God has seen you
admit you have spent your entire life
waiting there at the seventh station of the via crucis
sticking out your surreptitious foot to trip up God
admit that this action sums up perfectly your whole existence
admit it and ask forgiveness to the Galilean God whom you have
                                                     toppled over
for the Galilean is now getting up piece by piece and how he looks
                                                          at you
and looks at you and forgives your tripping and loves you
and he offers all his blood for you alone.

5

Blessed be the man called Simon the Cyrenian
for he was not out seeking God and yet he found him
on what mountain in what valley in what epiphany
in the disgrace in the disgrace of God Himself
he was merely passing by when they thrust the cross upon his shoulders
blessed be that simple soul beneath the cross
for he wanted to escape but now no longer wanted to
for he was seeking no one and he found God
in the disgrace in the disgrace of God Himself.

6

How easily he could have marched radiantly to the sacrifice
with illuminated eyes with his deity on display
                                                    how
how easily yet he chose to drag himself along like a damned one
yet he chose every stone of the way from all eternity
the exact tone of each insult and every blow he chose
why then why just for the sake of love alone
the Love which moves the sun and the other stars
formed each blob of spit exactly from all eternity.

7

The feet of pain are blood but oh its crown
its crown of shining stars the queen of God
glitters above the celestial hosts
blessed be all the pain of the world when accepted as the will of God
                                                    beloved be pain
hallowed and glorified be pain forever more amen
for God presents it to his christs
and He Himself comes down to put on his feet of blood
and He Himself crowns pain high above the celestial hosts
with the stars of the sacred Holy Trinity.

8

The way of Christ was thwarted by a woman
an exhalation with a cloth of white
the whole procession stopped and time stood still
her gesture took the stars aback completely
in an instant of eternity she fell upon her knees
please let me cleanse the visage of my Lord

Jesus pressed the cloth against his blood-stained face
and mumbling thank you gave her back the veil
those thanks still belonged to eternity
only when the woman raised a chalice to Jesus
on that signal time resumed its normal course
the stars and the procession resumed their movement
the soldiers spilled the chalice and the Pharisees
please let us soil the visage of our Lord
not much remained now in that face to soil
the woman turned back home spread out the veil
and thunderstruck she fell before the visage of her Lord
time once again stood still as she kissed eternity's face
eternity's lock of hair wide-open eyes and forehead
no one knows the name she went by in the realm of time
for all eternity her name will be Veronica.

9

If any man will come after me
let him take up his daily cross and follow me with cheerful face
because I myself am that cross and that cheerful face
is the face which I imprinted on Veronica's veil
which after me will be restored to life.

10

The place called Calvary
is a hill as bald as a human skull
death lost its locks and tresses long ago
and now goes dancing naked to the rhythm of its bones
on the hilltop destined for the Son of God
the place of the skull is a naked slope

that reeks of carrion and last year's flowers
it's a stormy crag where the wind goes whistling
where the demons of desolation howl
where the guardian vultures of the Palestinian sky
trace large concentric circles up above
my good sir here we are this is the place
what do you think of the setting for your glorification
have a swig now man it's wine with myrrh
its effect is comforting hypnotic anesthetic
it was recommended in the Book of Proverbs
give strong drink to the wretched and those of heavy heart
so that drinking they remember their miseries no more
his lordship does not care for this refreshment
he prefers to breathe the flowers of last year
he prefers his Father's chalice with the taste of carrion
he prefers to dance with his skull with no anesthesia
and just like that to whistle through his very bones
to fly over his concentric remains way up above
all right then every man is free to die upon the cross
whatever way he chooses even more if he's a king
please now your majesty extend your regal arms
over the throne prepared by your two nations
so you can reign from Rome and from Jerusalem.

11

Society has conceived innumerable methods of execution
the refined poetic fantasy of legislators
and the desire for a worldwide display of exemplary punishment
have made common cause with the innate sadism of the masses
giving birth to the rack the dislocation of every bone
death by disembowelment scalding steam skinning

burning at the stake drowning in the mud burial of the living
but none of these devices was horrendous or refined enough
for the execution of the man who bears every crime of humanity
the Jews were used to death by lapidation burning at the stake
                                                       decapitation
deaths too sweet too short too beautiful for Jesus
think about the classical beauty of bonfires at noon
it was the Romans' whose method was the best of all
a death reserved for slaves and vile foreigners
for Christ the crucifixion was a providential synthesis
the body nailed to the cross contracted from head to feet
producing a widespread tetanization from feet to head
the early and the later wounds were all inflamed together
the lungs exploded in the head and the head within the heart
from a physical point of view the anguish was unbearable
the abundant loss of blood insured in passing
a burning thirst which was felt by all the body
the entire body then became a cross unto itself
the timing of the pain was perfect for a lingering death
it is worthwhile now to note some ornamental details
dogs drew near to lap up every single drop of blood
the nimble ones leaped up to gnaw upon his feet
while his head served the urchins as a target for their stones
even the vultures dared to feed upon the living dead
no doubt the crucifixion was the most appropriate death the only one
for the priest who chose to suffer every sorrow of the universe
and to die every death in one alone.

1 2

Come hither king of the Jews off with your clothes once and for all
you wouldn't want to die in formal dress wearing the sacred mantle

we have come to take your measurements
we're the tailors of eternity the artists of the holy cross
something you should know of this if you were once a carpenter
before consecrating yourself to the sublime profession of royalty
Christ the King lies naked on the cross
his first contact with that eternal wood is a sudden flash of bliss
the executioners take the measure of that naked suit
flesh-color white as snow transparent which he will wear forever
Jesus stretches out to let them drive in nails until the end of time
oh Father the hour is at hand the moment has arrived
the fullness of time is upon us now
before closing his eyes in a reflex from blind terror
Jesus gazes for an instant at the sky a perfect blue
that poor symbol of himself which at the sound of the first hammer
will be stained with red and black the sweetest light
of the kingdom of this world the final sun that poor symbol
of himself that will die with him this midday night
now his right hand the one which calmed the seas the restorer to life
now comes the mighty nail now comes the mighty hammer
the blow is like his mind itself exploding
a groan both sweet and clear cries out a duo with the hammer
his blood proceeds to splash his executioners
and now the left hand what a stubborn hand
you'll see how well we stretch you now the ropes and oh my Father
they have dislocated his arms his knees are shaking madly
what stubborn legs they do not stretch enough
now you'll see how we can make you rise to the occasion
once again the ropes more dislocation and the bones what crackling
forgive them Father for they know not they are Jesus
oh Father oh my Father the Psalms cry out a duo with the hammer
with the tools of his own craft they are crucifying him
his mind does nothing but explode in his hands and in his feet

and each blow splatters it all red against the darkened midday sky
now he is sewn to the wood now the ropes exalt him
while the upright cross approaches verticality
the trumpets of the temple mount with the bleating of the sheep
those trumpets know not what they do because they are prophetic
they are heralding throughout the world the world's salvation on
the holy cross.

13

In the midst of the earth the Cross was raised for the first time
the base remained immobile but the top was quaking
the crowned head of Jesus was vibrating
Jesus let loose a ghastly cry all his wounds flew open
the heavenly angels flickered out around the holy Face
and then brusquely lit up again invisible above the cross
where they could look on God who could not look at them
and like a dream of God the Holy Church
all bathed in tears came flowing from his blinded eyes.

14

The INRI is
the identity card of the Word incarnate
the password which eternity exchanges with time
the first reaction of time confronted with eternity
the essential misunderstanding between man and God
the want of clarity of human existence
the greatest truth and lie ever inscribed
Pilate's mind enclosed within the mind of Caiaphas
Satan's star-spangled sky within the earth
God banished from paradise by the human race

the earth crowned by thorns on the heights of heaven
the gospel of pain preached by its own initials
the briefest complete language ever known
the rainbow reflected in the tears of Virgin Mary
the radiant aureole emitted by matter
when the blood of God makes contact with the dust
INRI INRI behold how that insane word
has begun to take flight towards eternity.

15

Indeed the dogs are coming to lick his blood
indeed if John didn't scare them all away they would bite his feet
indeed he is covered by flies which nobody scares away
indeed the tetanus cramp is crushing his thorax
indeed he tries to raise himself upon his feet to breathe
the air where is the air it has disappeared from all Judea
indeed he is devoured by thirst and water exists no longer
indeed the urchins bring their stones to hurl them at the target
and they would if John did not disperse them
indeed the threatening vultures are approaching
and only because of the growing darkness they disappear
indeed the night is falling in the midst of day
indeed a swarm of flies encircles him
indeed within the very core of darkness
the eternal Splendor of the Father eternal fades away.

16

To those who seek the Infinite on their own account
let it be known
that the object of their noble and erratic search

has already been found upon a cross
on the Friday of Nisan in the outskirts of Jerusalem
that cross would come to be the horizon of his revelation to the
entire world
the pilgrims of his Immensity are hereby notified that the search is over
inasmuch as its object has been fully identified
under the name of Jesus Christ of Nazareth
only starting from the aforementioned crucified the search for the
infinite God is possible
only within Jesus can the Absolute be explored
let it be known to the fishermen of the abyss that outside of Jesus
the Infinite positively denies the splendor of his face
inasmuch as he has revealed it in a total and exclusive form
crowned with thorns for greater proof
outside of him they will only find the mirage of his abandoned ways
no one answers for the eternal salvation of the pilgrims
the searchers of the Infinite on their own initiative
are hereby notified that they are sought for by the Infinite
the rendezvous is scheduled for the sixth hour on the outskirts of
Jerusalem
little or nothing can be known besides that body
crucified on the Friday of Nisan
beyond the irradiation of that bleeding cross
the Infinite takes no responsibility
for absolutely anything at all.

17

And what would become of the world what of the Church
were it not for those poor old sickly and abandoned women who
sigh in the darkness
sweet cross sweet tree
                    gentle Jesus comfort me.

18

He was the most handsome of the sons of man
his face was eternity passing through the features of Virgin Mary
so softly shaped by the Holy Spirit since the creation of the world
his eyes were like seeing God like one sole infinite gaze
everyman saw himself in that wandering mirror of God
his forehead possessed the exact form of the firmament
his august head was a parable of infinite mercy
his lips the eternal whistling of the good shepherd
the cedars of Lebanon used to dream of his neck
his hair flowed down like the cascades of the Tigris and Euphrates
the hair of eternity seen in dreams
its color was of dark copper and undiscovered metals
his shoulders were designed especially for the cross
his breast was firm like the rock of his own Church
and it was made for the dying head of the crucified to rest upon
his laborer hands saw just as much as his eyes
his feet were indefatigable messengers of his heart
ah who could tell of so much beauty while it dies
vertical unrecognizable with no memory upon the cross.

19

Oh cross our only hope
visible scaffold invisible throne of the king of kings
precious and adorable tree adorned with regal purple
tree of life in the midst of paradise in shadows
tree with roots in the center of the universe
tree of the mountain at the summit of the two kingdoms
a king chants at your feet a God dies on your heights
tree of the victory over hell
the wind through your leaves sings the new canticle

of the new creation lying at your feet
noble tree in the midst of all the trees of light
no forest ever bore such leaves such flowers of paradise
tree whence life came out from death itself
tree you hold in the branches of your immensity
the ransom of the centuries like fruit of gold
tree with your root you crush the ancient dragon
tree in the form of a chalice where the earth is dreaming
of the course of its stars above man's history
tree of the river which greens the new heaven and earth
tree which is watered and flowered in the most precious blood
tree a Jacob's ladder where angels clamber up and down
tree which flowers in the midst of this vale of tears
tree most high priest the only hope of all the nations.

VII. The Seven Words

1

The Pharisees wagged their head with jurisprudence
how many times did we tell you that you would end up badly
the Sadducees shook their best head apologetically
you claimed to have a kinship with the Most High
well then relinquish the unnecessary form of the cross and assume
                              the form of your kinship
transform yourself into a radiant and blinding cloud over your own
                                            INRI
into a species of celestial rainbow hovering over Jerusalem
then we will acknowledge you as King of the Jews
look he is not turning into the light of the Most High but on the
                                          contrary
he insists on dying and dying as the most doggish of all delinquents.

2

Now the convict exclaims to the face of heaven
Father forgive them for they know not what they do
he has requested not a fulminating ray but a lulling one
from heaven which will soothe them and this ray arrives
a blessed and gentle ray forgiving all the crucifiers
verily verily the absolute love for one's enemies
is the world upside down in his agonizing eyes

from the depths of his kingdom he begs forgiveness for his deicides
who know not what they do oh hapless human condition
they know not the immensity of their own action
they have less power to do themselves harm
than has Jesus to do them good for the perfect crime
which transforms them into loves of Jesus Christ.

3

Ah what a sweet revenge on his executioners
to forgive them
          to convert them
                    to transport them into paradise
and to wipe away their tears for all eternity.

4

There are three crucified men on Golgotha
one offers salvation one accepts it one disdains it
the history of salvation has had a prompt beginning
the thief on the left cries out to the INRI that if he is so kingly
then undertake the total liberation of these three prisoners of the
                                establishment
the other one hushes him and says to the INRI whom no one sees
remember me my Lord when thou comest into thy Kingdom!
and now the invisible King answers from the cross
verily I say unto thee today thou shalt be with me in paradise
verily a stupefied silence fills the other world and this one too
by faith alone the mountains are about to plunge into the sea
by faith alone the gates of paradise begin to open wide
one of the crucified believes that the other keeps a kingdom
                              underneath his wounds

that he hides the other world beneath his sores
and through the open mouth of his own wounds the thief acclaims
                                        remember me my Lord
ah there is not such faith in all the world as those very wounds
no prophet compares with those gaping holes of blood and light
through which the history of salvation makes its historical apparition
there is no Peter rock who can compare with that poor Dimas
                                        glorified this day
by accord between two dying men from cross to cross
a highwayman has just assaulted heaven in the dark
he has just robbed his God in articulo mortis
and he is the archangel Gabriel of the agony of God
that very scoundrel yes the last begin to be the first
like a thief in the night a good thief has become the smuggler of
                                        paradise.

5

Cross of the wicked thief horrible cross
neither accepted
                nor well used
                                nor robbed from the heart of Christ
just crucified by its furious man
next to Christ without Christ
that pitch-black wood with neither face nor glory
that cross with no paradise today
                tomorrow
                                maybe never
that cross of the wicked thief damnable cross.

6

What has the good thief seen on the adjoining cross
he has seen the inexpressible majesty
he has seen the incomprehensible divinity of
the Lamb of God
in his strangled eyes he has seen the loveable triumphant omnipotent
pain-supporting splendor of
the worm of God Himself amid the darkness.

7

If you are the King of Israel et cetera
if you are the Son of God come down et cetera
Jesus opens his exhausted eyes
he gazes on those eyes of rabbinical gaze
he shakes off his cross like a nightmare
that once might have stuck to his golden wings
he shakes off his wounds like a bad memory
of the years he passed among mankind
the wounds take flight like radiant birds
Jesus spreads his arms wide open in apologetic form
he flies over Calvary he is sheer light
he has descended from the cross he has climbed above the INRI
he is the sun he is an angel no doubt he is a king
he is God Himself perched above the scaffold
awaiting the reactions of mankind
the reactions of mankind are very slow
at first a somber terror which is quite understandable
then the dialectic reason and its reasons
Caiaphas claims that Beelzebub is mixed up in the affair
a transfiguration of the prince of darkness
Annas supports this theological interpretation

with the weight of years and lifelong experience
the experts mention an extrasensory illusion
collective hallucination a clever dream
the final trick of the dying impostor
the form taken by his death in the Mediterranean culture
Pilate suspects some Jewish plot against the metropolis
the truth and what is truth
once more everything is identical to itself
with or without a king Calvary is Calvary
no the history of salvation did not follow that path
Jesus remained in agony until the end of the age
because he was the Son of God he chose to keep on dying
he did not descend from the cross for it was his throne
out of love he did not fling his wounds to the seven winds
because he was truly a king he did not shake off his crown of thorns
like an evil thought
his divinity was the agony and he began to agonize more deeply
than ever
the facts nevertheless allow us to assume
that the reactions of mankind would be identical to themselves
more than ever let us kill the giver of life
let us kill Life upon the cross at once.

8

The sky withdraws into itself
the voice of the crucified sounds as if he were speaking
through the wounds of his hands through his whistling hollows
at his feet stands the mother crucified within herself
she must be stripped of everything even of that whistling
which is not the son of anyone because it is heavens that withdraw
that whistling calls her woman as if speaking from abroad

those who are about to die on the cross simply say my mother
the mothers of the crucified love to be called that way
how sweet would sound that whistling oh my mother from the INRI
but the receding heaven just calls her woman
as if speaking from abroad just woman
behold thy son
then the whistling points at John and looks at John and says
behold thy mother and he gives her to John as mother
the mother is the bequest of the receding heaven
the mother understands and suffers for she is the mother of heaven
and John is just a nice young man from earth
oh mother this exchange between heaven and earth
her motherliness crucified within her is crying
her cry will breed for her the sons from far abroad
those orphan johns and sinners who will be her Christs
that is why between mother and son the sky is exchanging signals
that is why between heaven and earth the angels sing Alleluia
although heaven recedes and its mourning cries abroad
rejoice all creatures of heaven and earth for now they have a mother
rejoice the sons of no one for now they are the sons of someone
at last the forsaken have their own virgin mother
rejoice the leprous children of God for their mother is like the snow
at last the hardened sinners have a mother in common with God
rejoice poor angels for now they have a queen
Adam and Eve have a mother at last
even Judas if he wished would have the sweetest mother
rejoice all the Christs of the world born beneath the cross
for their mother is the most beautiful among women.

9

Mother says John
I thought it impossible to love you more
but now that I have just been born
now that I have begun to multiply by endless millions
now I see that our love begins to lose itself in the infinite
under the form of the Church which loses itself
in the infinite under the form of the celestial Jerusalem.

10

Far from nature to remain indifferent
while its very author is in agony
the least that it can do is conceal its eyes
the earth is covered by a darkling mantle
which lends to Calvary a pious air of unreality
and to the language of the thieves a puzzling sound
far from the sky to remain translucent
when men have cast their shadow on the holy Face
the stars whose forms are signs of Christ himself
insist on being present on this night of the universe
the sun on the contrary at the sixth hour must die away
the synagogue of Satan must be darkened
far from Spring to go about fashioning flowers
when its radiant loved one dies away in the darkness
the moon has played its part it has risen in the East
and swiftly has concealed the sun that wishes to see nothing
the sun is but a ring an aureole of disseminated flames
a perfect symbol of the Word which now is dying
Calvary is illuminated only by the stars
which emit an agonizing blood-stained light
the darkness yields a widespread fear in all of Israel

there is no fire capable of lighting up this somber night
the offences at the foot of the cross fall dead in all this silence
men have clambered to the rooftops where they gaze upon the sky
and moan
the birds fly low and plunge to earth
Pilate and Herod tremble and take counsel with their seers
the blood of the beheaded lambs begins to bleat
scores of repentant Jews turn their eyes towards the cross
now the ring around the sun displays a supernatural red
the birds keep flying low and topple over
they fall dead at the foot of the cross a veritable symbol
nobody knows of what but still a veritable symbol
the sun which is a veritable symbol of Jesus Christ
contemplates those three crosses and conceals its eye of fire
and with the pallid hands of the moon covers its face
leaving only its aged and yellow hair spread out
which the sidereal wind disperses towards the infinite.

11

Some onlookers are passing by and stop
with their empty eyes
to contemplate this eclipse of the sun in a crucifix
the star-filled sky in a tear
a most curious spectacle brought by satellite
a curious transmission from the other world
a mute interrogation about nothing
some inquisitive people gaze and yawn
with the mouth of the dead one
come on Joe
so much ado for a crucified man
turn off the light let's go.

12

There on high Jesus is wrapped in greater darkness than all of Israel
God abandons him to the infinite solitude of sinners
face to face with the empty heaven he prays as if God did not exist
and a verse ascends in prayer to his voice asking Eloi
Eloi my God my God why hast thou forsaken me?
God is a man as abandoned as if he were not God
who asks a God so absent as if He didn't exist
it's the bottom of the bottomless chalice that he drinks now in the
                                                                darkness
it's his love and our love which ascends in prayer to his voiceless
                                                                voice
when he has nothing left and is more nude than death itself
he must still be denuded even of his Father who is in heaven
heaven is closed and No One answers him in the darkness
he offers his abandonment to the One who has abandoned him and
                                           in the infinite Absence
the Son touches bottom in the abysm of the incarnation
he has taken on this sinful flesh cutting off his bridges
leaping forth with his poor human heart towards nothingness
and becoming the very heart of the sinful darkness which clamors
                                                          from below
why hast Thou forsaken me my God as if Thou did not exist.

13

He raised his eyes unto the heavens and saw himself
infinite glorious and smashed to bits
in the mirror of his Most Holy Trinity.

14

Jesus is the void of God over the darkened earth
over that human night shines the last splendor of the INRI
those last forsaken men whom life has cast away into his holy agony
can still be reached by the most crucified voice that whispers in the
dark
thou shalt be with me in paradise today.

15

The fifth word I thirst is not addressed to anyone in particular
he is not asking for water he is only offering information
of a strictly impersonal nature concerning his ghastly state
he thirsts for water all his being cries for water
he thirsts for the love of Judas Pilate Annas and Caiaphas
the cross has a parching thirst for all who gaze at it
the tremendous truth is that he fell in love with everyone
that Glory stands absolutely in no need at all
yet our poor hearts are everything for him
I thirst I thirst so badly cries the Glory from the cross
as if we ourselves were the water of paradise he looks at us.

16

After tasting the vinegar Jesus said
it is fulfilled
all the prophecies have been more than accomplished
at last the creation of the world has reached full term
at last the chosen people know the reason why
at last its endless exodus is over
at last the mystery of Jerusalem has been deciphered
at last the victim and the priest become as one upon the cross

at last salvation descends like a dream over the Vatican
at last the Summa Theologica can be written down
at last the woodsman in the forest is a woodsman
and man at last man infinitely surpasses man
at last all human work is holy holy holy
at last all crafts can spring from the heart of God
the sense of suffering is revealed at last in all its immensity
at last the cradle of the new-born infant is a mystery
at last the man and the woman who lie together are a supernatural
mystery
at last the seven sacraments begin their mad career towards paradise
at last the lives of saints have broken loose
and prepare to invade the world with their stories
it is fulfilled cried out the Messiah when on his tongue
the vinegar accomplished the last of all its prophecies
heaven at last has been finished in its motionless light
and descends like a dream over the earth.

17

Jesus one last look
through his crossed eyes through his beautiful priestly eyes
eternity is coming upon us with inconceivable speed
at last his eyes have closed and all of a sudden God appears to
God.

18

The hour of his glorification comes
his body is as pale now as the moon itself
his arms like priests have opened wide
with the last light of his spirit

he has raised his crowned head
as though he were raising the entire firmament
and has cried out
Father
        into thy hands I commend my spirit
and he bowed his head
                        and gave up the ghost
the firmament falls as if struck by lightning
earthquakes come bursting forth out of themselves
the mouth of the dead begins to speak
the archangels cry out as best they can
Jesus tears his soul out of his body
and into the outstretched hand of his Father
he deposits
the translucent offering of his soul
the cry of his own blood in the abysms
the chalice now perpetual
which the Father holds trembling out of pure light
the heavens of the heavens are aflame
yes the hand of the Father
with that soul in his hand
trembles
around that brilliant host
a band of angels crowds and whirls together
on Calvary the day died out completely
over the body of God that host in shadow
which hell examines feverishly
while only Mary's tears
illuminate the night of all the ages.

19

History tells of some beautiful deaths
the noble gesture of Socrates
that still endures in the light of Attica
slowly imbibing his hemlock
or the first martyr Stephen his angelic face
contemplating above the clouds the glory of Jesus Christ
or those legions of men women children of Jesus Christ
who cried out in the face of death Viva Christ the King
yes history records triumphal deaths
but Jesus Christ the leprous Christ the love
the afflicted by God the priest and victim
could not die crying Viva Christ the King
he died of an immense and somber death
the total death the dreadful death of man
the first-born son of sin
Jesus the first-born son among the dead the savior
he did not see the Christ while he was dying
he reached the great abyss completely naked
out of sheer love forsaken between heaven and earth
he suffered one by one every forsaken death
the cry of the sickly the terror of the perverse with neither God nor
law

the shot of the suicide the torment of the assassinated virgin
the most handsome of all the sons of man
from love alone he willed to die the horror of death itself
the infinite dying
so death with its own eyes could look on God
so death could whisper

Long live

Christ

the King.

VIII. Death

1

Jesus was only a rumor for him until last night
a picturesque note on the Hebrew landscape
where he passes through on the way to his ascent
a centurion is familiar with executions
and personally he never presumed to be over-sensitive
but that crucified man that beast in agony oh what majesty
when he implored forgiveness from heaven for his executioners
all the centurion's knowledge of human nature crumbled
his eyes were glued to that blood-stained face
he was on the verge of crying as never in his childhood
when the crucified lifted up his head crowned with thorns
and the afternoon light seemed to revolve about that gesture
and the moribund clamored to his Father and the earth shook
the centurion hurled his lance far away and shouted with a new and
                                                     incognito voice
blessed be the all-powerful God Father of Jesus the Christ
blessed be Jesus for truly he is the Son of God
his cry converted some of the soldiers and two or three Pharisees
his cry came down from Calvary racing headlong through the valley
                                                     prophesying
the Savior of the world is dead long live the Savior.

2

One single man suffered crucifixion
on those three crosses of Golgotha
one single man invaded the Roman Empire
suffering countless casualties in the endeavor
one single man defended the Empire from every invasion
and met his death once and again on every front
the black plague destroyed one single man in all of Europe
impossible though it was to bury such a multitude of corpses
one single man perished in the seven crusades
which that single man undertook for the love of his holy sepulcher
the French Revolution guillotined just one single man
one single man suffered the endless Soviet genocides
one single man fell fulminated in the First World War
the same who later fell in the Second and the Third
the mystical body of all human suffering
has one single head crowned by thorns.

3

The Good Shepherd passed away in the darkness of Golgotha
his lovely whistling wanders through the immensity of the night
searching for itself but all in vain
it finds only demons who imitate his whistling
I am the Good Shepherd and I know my sheep
know thyself poor soul in torment
the green pastures are absolutely empty
there is neither green nor grass but only stones and night
the wind beats down on that stony ground bearing only demons
who whistle where are you my ninety-nine lost sheep
I am the sheep lost in the eyes of the Good Shepherd
the Good Shepherd went astray and his white flocks

are no longer white they seek themselves at midnight
they are the immense black night where dreams go bleating
they are the green pastures gone astray from its sheep
where are my sheep moans the green nothingness
no one feeds on me for I am only stones
the pasture goes wandering through the immensity of the night
seeking itself in the midst of bleatings
it is a green bleating in torment which says oh Shepherd
no one here knows anyone the nights pass by
the demons the wind the pasture and the whistling pass by
come to restore a little order that there might be
one single sheepfold one single shepherd one single flock
that's what you promised before you went astray
find thyself Good Shepherd and whistle lovingly
but no there is no answer only the wind
only the demons whistle at midnight
only the wolves are howling off on the horizon
the Good Shepherd lost his way in the darkness of Golgotha.

4

Jesus is quite dead but a conscientious soldier
impales his dead rib with a lance like a ray of light
that prophetic ray of light wrenches from the bosom of the world's
                                                    salvation
blood and water water and blood John will repeat for centuries
for the entire Church is born of those two substances
all the vows of mutual love between the world and God
are made through that peerless mouth of the universe
where the angels of glory whistle in the darkness
the soldier kneels confessing that the Church is born
the Virgin feels her heart transfixed by that same lance

the soldier contemplates the open rib as though he were seeing God
God contemplates his holy mother through that open rib
God contemplates Saint John through his blood and water
those two substances are seven and they are called the sacraments
which set out from the open rib to conquer the world through Spirit
to conquer the world through matter.

5

The wound of the open rib of Jesus Christ
is a mystery of sorrow yet radiant with happiness
it's an endless coming and going of saints and angels
it's the breach that clears the way to paradise
it's the only eternal wound for it will live again unchanged
it's the blue glimpsed through the clouds of the Apocalypse
it's the open sesame of the Eucharist's intoxication
it's the belvedere of the secrets of the sacred heart
it's the only window authorized by the Holy Spirit
to ponder the solution to the problem of evil in the universe
it's the only solution to the problem of pain
it's the mouth of God who breathes the world into his inner self
it's the concavity of the rock where dwells the mystic dove
where the apostolic Church lives and will take to flight
on Pentecost when the agreed-on signal comes.

6

The tree of the cross
is naked and blood-stained with neither fruit nor flowers
the wind on its only branch sighs the weeping of the infinite
yet that tree is more beautiful than the cedars of Lebanon
more beautiful than the golden trees of the Hesperides

that tree of death
has God entangled on its only branch
and the tree of paradise lost
and the tree of paradise gained
stretch out their fruits and flowers towards that tree of death.

7

A crucifix is the immensity of the love of God
that hangs from any wall
                 painted
                           or pocket size
just open any dwelling of the history of salvation
and the immensity appears descending from the heavens
and God casually appears in his mirror.

8

These are the thousand wounds of Christ the pilgrim
one alone can save the whole world
for example wound number 171 of the flagellation in the middle of
                                      his chest
who knows its path through history?
ah the life and the miracles of that single wound
in its passage through Byzantium Toledo Santiago
what an endless chain of saints have dozed away
in the shadow of its outspread wings
how many sweet Madonnas have its colors painted
in the light of its restless pilgrim eyes
history will never know the debt it owes that wound
how many lepers its compassionate hand has cleansed
what host of human footsteps have not been lost in God

by virtue of that single wound and all its labyrinths
what multitude of faces have not turned the other cheek
for the sake of its celebrated patience
what pure syllogisms have not been caviled at
by the intelligence of that single wound
on the highroad to Damascus
what a flood of conversions are ascribed to it
how many wounds has that wound not cured
ah the history of pectoral wound one hundred and seventy-one
of the peregrine body of Jesus Christ.

9

His head now lies upon his mother's knees
his feet upon the knees of Magdalene
in the perishing light of an eternal day
stars around them are about to appear
Mary covers with kisses his disfigured face
and Magdalene his wounded feet with tears
they cover him with kisses slowly slowly
two three eternities follow one another
they cleanse him with more care than were he still alive
then Mary takes away the crown of thorns
ever so cautiously as if his head might be restored to life by a sudden
                                                                        pain
with curiosity the universe observes that bluish crown
the wounded rib looks on like an abyss
Mary washes and cleans the face of the world
the starry night wears on before reaching his feet
before reaching the tearful eyes of Mary Magdalene
the earth just like a mother bids farewell
endless kisses for Jesus and adieu.

10

Mother
even God willed to sleep in your arms of a Mother
even God willed to die in your Pietá.

11

The sepulcher at last for God the Son
Joseph of Arimathea lays out the body
God drives away the flies which pester God
God Himself keeps watch over his own face
God looks at himself in that mirror and sees himself so dead
so still so Jewish such a total failure
piously God bends over his remains
God is well that way after so much
death and so much suffering God is now at peace
Joseph of Arimathea has earned a place in heaven
and God the Son has earned that heart of living rock.

12

This night of all the nights the most profound
the nightliest of all the nights on earth
this Good Friday night flows from the holy sepulcher as one
and fills up space and time completely
with the infinite nocturnality of God
this is the night when animals
have a touch of the human when the plants
attain the power of reason and then lose it
this is the night when matter
knows itself equal to God that dead man
and the distant suns of other lonely systems

radiate a black light and all the trees
frighten away their birds because
they feel a hanging Judas in their branches.

13

I turn my back on you and go astray in the night
says Peter as he flees along the byways
covered by ashes and by deprecations
I go astray in these airs of oblivion
while you go on staring into my eyes
death oh Christ has already closed your eyelids
yet you stare at me through death and hell
you gaze on me your blood just looks at me
that cross looks into me just like an open eye
throughout the centuries you stare at me
with myriads of nocturnal eyes yes you the lamb
thrice slaughtered by my denying soul
while roosters crow in heaven
Christ forgive me and stare at me no more.

14

This is the Sabbath the most empty day
this is the Sabbath of nothingness
when the Lord God rested from his own existence
when men give thought to nothing
when history proclaims not one step further
for the body of God now rests in peace.

15

Death hovers haughtily above the holy sepulcher
like a dragon guarding its treasure beneath the rock
without the faintest idea of the speed of the dead man to whom she
will give birth.

16

The soul of Jesus that incorporeal sun
descends to the abode of the dead
God's rainbow explodes above the abyss
Jesus resplendent
passes through the Avernus of the blind
at last it will be known who we are
they are the dead the dead of so many ages
the judgment the judgment of the imprisoned spirits
at last we will know who you are oh sun foretold
Jesus is identified by his intensity
it's you it's you clamors the countless death
Adam and Eve kneel down in adoration
Abraham and Jacob and Moses and David adore
their own incorporeal blood in the sun of Christ
Joseph of Nazareth his embrace seems to last forever
and finally the good thief verily I said unto thee
his soul conserves the gesture of the crucifixion
freedom endless freedom for the imprisoned spirits
where oh death where is thy victory
Jesus now approaches the abyss
his gaze is terrifying above that darkness
what have we to do with you howl the Lucifers
now the doors of eternity are closing
now only the curse of Judas can be heard

now the well of the night remains immobile
in the light of death and hell
our immensity at last has been discovered.

17

Satan Satan
who would say you missed the mark completely
who would say that you were providential
it can be said you saved the world from Satan
when you corrupted Judas and Caiaphas
when with all of hell you stormed the Sanhedrin
when you possessed in body and soul the carpenters of the crucifixion
when you pierced the feet and hands of your poor victim
when you roared your song of victory over the entire world
this is how in your blind and somber manner
you made your exact and necessary gift to the salvation of the world
and delivered the sons of Eve from Satan.

18

This Sabbath night is barely night
the birds awaken the trees before their time
the stargazers don't know what's going on
the children stay awake with no fear in the dark
this night can barely manage to dissemble
this night can wait no longer and to the world proclaims
that it is neither night nor day but just
a shadow which holds its breath
and the bashful fringe of the glorious tunic of
the most infinite Day of all the days.

IX. The Resurrection

1

Beneath the moonlight everything is quiet
the Jewish guards are keeping watch in groups of seven
they fiercely guard the dead against himself
within the tomb under the shroud
lies the body of Jesus encompassed by its own light
two angels stand in adoration at his head and feet
the soul of Jesus comes back from Avernus
together with the souls of patriarchs and prophets
and passes through the rock of the sepulcher
and shows them the wounds of his dead body
each wound displays the bottom of its own abyss
the saints of Israel look on with loving awe
they raise up disembodied cries
now Jesus takes his tortured body up
to the summit of heavens with no moving at all
and presents it to the Father's loving eyes
the Father Himself is deeply moved
when He embraces that flaming host which comes from the world
below
that supreme suffering His consubstantial Son
the Father seems to say not that much was needed
now the dead body rests in the sepulcher

it must submit to a treatment that borders on glory before returning
to life
the angels must restore to him the sacred matter
which the passion dispersed among the elements of the world
through the lashes the fists the tattered rags
and the wood and Veronica's veil fluttering in the four winds
for the sake of the world that matter must remain dispersed
it must be scattered by the seven winds
and simultaneously be restored to its glorious owner
the world is now a relic but the body must remain intact
because in a few more seconds that body

oh my God
four
three
oh God that body
two
one
that body oh God
has now
returned to life!

2

Jesus
henceforth your name will not be
waste land
nor
the leper is dying
nor
accursed in you the light of the universe
no
henceforth your name will be

the home of man
and
the other face of the sun is born
and
my love my love eternity my love.

3

The soul of Christ resplendent came alone
glorious as a ray from heaven it traversed the rock
he made his own what was his own and like a blow of pure glory
he rushed into his body which rose up in pure glory
operation soul-body-glory took place all at once in God's bosom
it took place in the tomb itself and in the very self of God
all of a God will be man for ever and ever
this man now moves in glory now emerges from his shroud
like a God suddenly awakened he rises like pure light
how sweetly does the living rock feel itself traversed
that stone is now used to the passing of the spirits
but this is something else it's a body like itself yet of the purest glory
meanwhile an angel from heaven flings itself upon the sepulcher
and rolls the stone away to let the world take a look at its inside
the angel sits on the stone like the doorman of eternity
ah this poor stone has not yet recovered from this cosmic morning
this morning earth and heaven pass right through her as if nothing
the sepulcher is open and empty like a flashing void
the guards are toppled over by so much lightning from the other world
and in this world a momentary pause while the new Jesus
prepares to meet his loved ones
prepares to make his debut in human history.

4

The first one Jesus looks for is his mother
what a violent and divine and human wish
to embrace his own mother with his own glory
for this one embrace he was dying to return to life
the night was still black when the Virgin set foot on the pavestone
her son was teledirecting those footsteps from the other world
from the glory her son was guiding them
the Virgin was creating the first via crucis of history
she seemed to be in search of a lost object
from time to time she bent to touch the stones or kiss the dust
the fourteen footprints of Christ were the objects of her adoration
her heart never erred
in the darkness her lips always came upon that blood
more certainly than had it shone in splendor on the road
the daylight suddenly encircled her
the day was Jesus Christ surrounding her
the king of all the days for its own queen
Jesus enfolded his mother in his infinite light
the mother embraced God her son as only a mother does
as though all of creation like a mother was embracing its own Creator
not even the angels can measure the length of that one embrace
the angels of the Son bowed down before their queen
while far off in the East a tenuous sun was dawning
like a toy sun like a pale emblem of the only true light.

5

These vales of tears dawned in all their greenery
glorious as a dream they have appeared
after the longest night in history
nobody now remembered all these vales of tears

they were ashes and dust beneath the fog
these vales of God this morning
are no longer vales of tears but morning dew
the morning star presaged it
a drop of sun hangs from each green fiber
at the tip of each fiber the sun has appeared
telling fabulous lies
an incredible history yet true
born of a virgin mother crucified and resurrected
the sun repeats that it has undergone a thousand hardships to reach
the zenith of each fiber
to make the vale its own it has passed
through perils never heard of for the sun
through nights whose story is unsuitable for a self-respecting valley
the entire valley believes its fabulous tales
the valley is the best proof of itself
I am green therefore my dream is true
the flowers are its INRI made of gold
the lily of the valley claims I am the empirical proof of the resurrection
the morning demonstrates the morning to itself
the valley to the valley says I'm evident
glorious as a dream these vales of tears have met the dawn
the valleys of the tears of God Himself.

6

As soon as the morning star appeared
Joanna Mary of Cleophas Salomé and Magdalene
collected all the balsam of Jerusalem
all the perfumes of the world traveled in their amphoras
the early birds woke up by the fragrancy
every Sunday of history has been the same since then

the women headed towards the dead man not the resurrected
love is stronger than death
they did not fear the guard about which they knew nothing
they only knew about the rock that sealed the sepulcher
ah how the world separates the great death from the great life
the women's anxiety did not belong to metaphysics but only to mechanics
love also has its very own mechanics
love also has surprises of its own
the stone had been removed beyond mechanics
the guards disseminated all seemed dead
among the wet bushes lay the victims of lightning
the women saw the sepulcher wide-open like an abyss
the Magdalene a prisoner of love in the world of mechanics
cried robbery and raced to Peter with the feet of wind
which rose up all at once in solidarity with the Spirit
the others were afraid and yet attracted by the sepulcher
the burning mouth of the abysm beckoned them
and there they found two priests with raiment like the snow
why seek you the living among the dead
wasn't this foretold by him in due time
tell the Pope that Jesus is infinitely alive
and doing honor then to their angelic condition they promptly
disappeared
in the air of the resurrection so astoundingly luminous.

7

John and Peter come flying at the news of the theft
not even dreaming of the Sunday they are flying through
John the younger first reaches the sepulchral abyss but
the prehistoric Church is already hierarchical
you first and after you and now inside

two things amaze them first the emptiness
a house a box a space can all be empty
but emptiness like this has not been seen before
they seem to see the nothingness to touch it like the exact form
of the body which is not there any longer
of all the possible ways for a thing not to be there
no one has ever seen a Not like this before
it is the most fulminating Not in the history of creation
the next surprise is a little uniqueness of this Not
the underclothing of the resurrection
the neatly folded bandages the shroud wrapped up
lying like mysteries in their respective places
body snatchers are never so meticulous
ah the order of the light to undress itself like lightning
leaving the garments in their proper place
blessed be those who believed the women after only seeing
the radiant emptiness of the tomb and
the outfit of resurrected death in order.

8

May all the stars be lit in the fullness of the day
may the star of Bethlehem become our sun
may the sun become the moon of these pale kingdoms
because the Christ who prefigured the sun has risen
because this morning the sun has risen beyond the symbol
it is born in the East and the sun flees through the darkness
may the sun dare to gaze into the eyes of Christ
and not be ashamed of blinking or going blind
and you our poor Jerusalem who knew not how to love
radiant with light arise take off in flight
toward the city transparent as Christ which bears your name

passing over the terrestrial city of Rome
and who are those who fly like sky-borne clouds
and who have perched like doves upon our doorways
they are the other cities of creation which await
a ray of light of Christ to journey meekly
towards the time and place assigned to them by the history of salvation
you Babylonia even you are forgiven if you become
the flash the humblest flash of his resurrected eyes
and you Holy Mary the little handmaid of the Lord and queen of
all the angels
the burning sun to which you gave birth is now entirely yours
and now thou shall be crowned with a tiara of a dozen stars
eternally ashamed of themselves around your eternal beauty
may the mountains leap like new-born lambs over the earth
may the deserts exult under the rain and burst with wildflowers
may the ocean be finally shipwrecked in the eyes of Christ
may the course of the rivers trace the emblem of their new Adam
and you the bones dispersed by the dust of so many centuries
you the children of dust the flowers of autumn that grow by the
roadside
ah the world is made of the dead more than of the living
may you sleep the brief and light sleep of oblivion
because the Face before which the earth and sky will disappear is
coming now
and the sea will deliver up its dead and Hades and the abysms
hark the trumpet of the angels of the resurrected
announcing that eternity has now begun.

9

Mary Magdalene strolls through the garden like a somnambulist
like the bride of the Song she roams and weeps like the beloved

her love whispers to her darkly that he is very near
Magdalene now is draped with dew
the flowers are opening all about her
the mystical roses open with a bursting sound
the veil has fallen from her head
her head of hair springs softly in the sunshine of the paschal world
when she turns her head to arrange her hair
in the precise angle of that proper women's gesture
she sees the radiant guardian angels of the tomb
but her reaction is the opposite of common mortals
she does not fall backwards before their glory
woman why dost thou weep a luminous spirit inquires
with the voice of many waters in accordance with his condition
and the love-struck woman blind from love
indulges in the luxury of confusing him with a passerby
who was out to breathe the air of the early morn
I know not where they have lain him she summarily replies
and treating the morning dialogue with the luminous spirit as over
she goes seeking her dead love in some other corner of the garden
even a chorus of all the archangels could not distract her
now still another figure dressed in white emerges from the bushes
and once again that question woman why dost thou weep
the whole world seems to be interested only in her weeping
as though there were no reason in this world for weeping
this new figure resembles the gardener of a parable
and in the light of the newborn day appears like smoke
however she is in no mood to recall the symbols of Jesus
nor to analyze the consistency of matter at the break of day
bound to the letter of her love she takes him for a simple gardener
who asks once again woman who is it you seek
and she assuming that the whole wide world must know whom she
                                                              refers to

replies if you hast carried him away
tell me where thou hast lain him so I can find him
how profoundly this loving blindness moves the dead man resurrected
with what a resurrected voice he whispers to her as she leaves
Mary!
oh holy God now Mary trembles more than the bride of the Song
of Songs
no one but Jesus can whisper her name like that from beyond the dead
and from beyond the dead she embraces his feet as on that earlier day
in the midst of one embrace and the other stands the very history
of redemption
Jesus who one day loved those kisses and tears on his historical feet
says to her touch me not to make her understand
the most sacred remoteness of the glory
in brief that he no longer enjoys his former existence
that even the most passionate love must analyze the consistency of
matter at the break of day
if you please life and death and resurrection must be distinguished
touch me not for I am not ascended to my Father yet
go tell my brethren I ascend unto my Father
and now as if the hour of ascension were at hand
he disappeared
the Magdalene was crying out of tender joy
the dew had spread itself upon her hair
her head of hair hung loosely in the glory of the sun
when the other women found her more alive than dead.

1 0

Two days ago says the Magdalene on this the third day
I bid farewell to him under the horror of the reddened cross
in yesterday's mirror I saw my hair all gray
today may hair is brown once more I blossom.

11

Jesus so much in love
has ventured forth in search of apparitions
he departs from Jerusalem disguised as a stranger
he travels incognito like a king who among his subjects
tries to find out the true state of his kingdom
the true state is appalling
Jesus prods two disciples of Emmaus to speak out
the travelers are sad and downcast in agnosticism
the stranger's ignorance surprises them
but man haven't you ever heard of Jesus
of what Jesus asks Jesus and he makes them tell the story of himself
from the point of view of agnosticism
of Jesus that beautiful dream of ours who died on the cross
the dream who walks with them proceeds with caution
everyone knows the danger in suddenly waking a human being
first a tug of the ears oh slow of heart
then the Scriptures it was written have you never read
the letters that the Holy Spirit sends you
and in conclusion the itinerary of salvation
the door to paradise is through a cross as it was written in
they have reached Emmaus and sir remain with us
why don't you eat with us and spend the night
potluck of course you understand
the night has fallen on the roads
we can see you're a prophet but don't abuse your tremendous eyes
Jesus oh what an actor he acts as if he's going on to who knows where
yet after a little coaxing he accepts their hospitality
they sit down at the table and when Jesus blesses when he breaks
it is thee thou art Jesus Christ arisen thou art oh
your gesture would reveal you among a billion people
nobody in the world could break the bread as you have done and

suddenly he vanished
they can worship only the light he left as he was going
like a lash of God in the darkened air
what prophet not a chance it had to be himself
was not our heart aflame within us
indeed their heart was all aflame when the landlady returned
where do we stand now are you two or three for supper
what's going on you also disappear
yes lady a very urgent message to communicate
the most important episode of universal history has just now come
to pass
though perhaps you do not realize it we're in another world
we're going to Jerusalem so thank you and adieu.

1 2

Remain with us for now the night is falling
in the heart of darkness you will reveal your name as if it were a
dream
and then like madmen we will awaken inside the very Sun.

1 3

He is the same and not the same as days before
he appears and disappears in thin air at his pleasure
his organism behaves like lightning
it goes through walls as if nothing
possessing all the properties of thought
he resembles a wanderer a forest or the wind sweeping over the
beaches
then suddenly the eyes the voice of always
he can regulate his glory as if to annihilate an angel
or to make it bearable to the eyes of a fisherman

what an ordeal for the glory to convince them
when it claims I am the carpenter recently crucified
these poor fishermen do not experience a total joy
even joy takes its time to reach the heart
the problem of the infinite is a problem of acclimatization
these poor men think they are dealing with a spirit
which for the resurrection of the flesh would mean a total failure
Jesus then must resort to exorbitant arguments
to concessions almost forbidden to a glorious body
exhibition of the wounds proofs of obscuration
I am the selfsame Jesus clamors that suppliant light
do you have anything to eat he asks them with a famished voice
and he devours a roast fish while they stare at him dumbfoundedly
like a magician who puts everything into his final number
let's see if anyone has ever seen a pure spirit gulping down a fish
look at these crucified wounds they are I my very self
my resurrected wounds are glorious but they are wounds
and the apostles submit to the wounds and the fish
ah the great events of life how slow they are to reach the heart
and the apostles let the infinite slip away slowly
through the dust of their sandals through their rustic clothing
through their Jewish heart their heart of stone.

14

Oh death where is thy victory
you were the conqueror the absolute the queen
of the night in the air of oblivion
you were the whore of darkness
the sexless one of the pitch-black chasm
that feasts on its own offspring
the leper of itself the filthiest

the coronated harpy of the universe
the rightful heir of sin
oh death where is thy victory
conquered by Jesus you are the most beautiful
overcome by him you are almost nothing
the virgin at the threshold full of light
she who kisses and then vanishes into the infinite
you are the mate of lightning and the naked one
impregnated by sunshine you are the illuminator
who perishes from light and disappears
oh death where is thy victory
Christ resplendent annihilated you
he has smitten your aged face of carrion
he has dragged through the dust your flowing locks
look at yourself in the mirror oh conquered one
now that you have become almost transparent
your kingdom is no more you are the shadow
of the sun over yourself oh almost nothing
oh virgin at the threshold bathed in light.

15

The risen Christ will land at any moment on these Galilean shores
meanwhile says Peter I'll go fishing and the other say me too
there they go plowing the waves of the world in their boat
that is unaware of being the apostolic Church
and now they cast their nets which are unaware
of being fishermen of men that species of the deep
the enormous star-clustered night has swiftly passed by
time and again the nets are empty oh what a night of misery
this night which is unaware of being the history of salvation
at dawn they glimpse upon the shore a man

a fugitive of the species from the deep
who cries to them as though the head of operation deep
cast your net on the right side and ye shall find
it is the break of day when everything can happen
and the truth is everything does happen the prophetic nets are filled
the heart of John looks closely at the alien chief
who knows so well the habits of the fish from the deep
and suddenly his heart cries out it's he it is the Lord
then Peter plunges into the water and swims to Jesus
and dripping with the deep he gets there first
Jesus has kindled a fire but he keeps silence
the miraculous catch is lying there at the feet of the Great Fisherman
and no one says a single word the silence is like the love of God
at the feet of the silence lie the fish of the love of God
then follow me and I will make you fishermen of men
that word now three years old returned to life this morning
the morning itself is silence and gestures like blowing on the coals
gestures like sharing of the bread and simple words like
bring the fish to the coals like come and eat and
that is all there is in the silence of the paschal morn
what on earth is involved in this glorious mystery
almost nothing almost everything the unheard-of candor
with which the glory of God is displayed in the new world
the everyday gestures transcended by eternity
so this is the Holy Christian Church the communion of saints
the forgiveness of sins the resurrection of the dead
so this is eternity in time some simple words
to work and to light the fire to fish and to fish the depths
with miraculous nets to catch the love of God
to eternalize the gestures of the holy day-to-day
and to march over the sands as if nothing
Christ has summoned his own to Galilee for all of this

nothing has happened here everything has happened
the immense starry night has happened swiftly over the deep
and the apostolic Church is about to return to life.

16

They have reached the summits of Galilee
the mountains take flight to see the Father
while the heavens recline to see the Son
heaven and earth bid farewell on the summit with a command
go ye therefore my infallible children and teach all the nations
baptizing them in my blood by the Holy Spirit
the risen Christ sends to tell all the world that he indeed has risen
he has risen he has risen the heavens are falling upon the Church
let the forests know it and bloom miraculously
let the ethereal tribes give the signal with their nets of gold
let all the electricity of the world notify it to the world
Christ has risen the news must be heralded from the highest peaks
be it spread by the demographic explosion of the planet
by the mouth of the dead by the new-born mouth by the mouths
                                                    which kiss
by hereditary transmission by contagion by cosmovision
rejoice the maternity wards and the lightnings and those who sleep
rejoice the laboratories and the kitchens and the mineral beds
let the cybernetics chant the Christ has risen
let all the computers explode from joy because within their memories
every bit of data of the center ring is already vibrating
let the swarms of ether whisper it in their own fashion
let loose this wandering cry over the highways and the stratosphere
let it appear in dreams and be heard in the kingdom come
let the Church shout it from the mountain tops and in the deep
let it explode inside the mind and may this sun

and the solar system and the Milky Way and the whole wide world collapse upon themselves for Christ has risen!